The Politics of Parenthood

The Politics of Parenthood

*Causes and Consequences of the
Politicization and Polarization
of the American Family*

Laurel Elder

and

Steven Greene

Cover photo credit: © Ryan Burke /iStockphoto.com

Published by State University of New York Press, Albany

For information, contact State University of New York Press, Albany, NY
www.sunypress.edu

Production by Diane Ganeles
Marketing by Michael Campochiaro

Library of Congress Cataloging-in-Publication Data

Elder, Laurel.
 The politics of parenthood : causes and consequences of the politicization and polarization of the American family / Laurel Elder and Steven Greene.
  p. cm.
 Includes bibliographical references and index.
 ISBN 978-1-4384-4395-9 (hardcover : alk. paper)
 ISBN 978-1-4384-4394-2 (pbk. : alk. paper)
  1. Parenthood—United States. 2. Families—United States. 3. Parenthood—United States—Public opinion. 4. Families—United States—Public opinion.
5. United States—Politics and government. I. Greene, Steven. II. Title.

HQ755.8.E367 2012
306.874—dc23   2011047985

10 9 8 7 6 5 4 3 2 1

To our parents: Carol and Richard Elder;
Hilde and Robert Greene

Contents

Tables and Figures

Tables

Figures

Acknowledgments

A book this long in the making means a lot of people to thank. We definitely need to start with the many friends and mentors in the Ohio State Political Science department, where we began our friendship—if not our collaboration. Paul Beck was the best adviser either of us could ask for in guiding us through our respective dissertations and later provided advice and support for this project. Likewise, Herb Weisberg was a tremendous mentor and adviser to both of us at Ohio State and in the early stages of this research. Other Ohio State faculty: Tom Nelson, Janet Box-Steffensmeier, Dean Lacy, William E. Nelson, Katherine Tate, Kira Sanbonmatsu, Aage Clausen, Gregory Caldeira, Elliot Slotnick, Lawrence Baum, and Samuel Patterson provided great guidance during our time there, as did Retta Semones. Our peers from Ohio State, especially Joe McGarvey, Stefanie Chambers, Jason Pigg, Pedro Magalhães, and Barry Burden also very much deserve recognition for being such supportive friends.

This book has been the result of numerous conference presentations as well as discussions with peers and colleagues. Among those most valuable in shaping and aiding our work, we would like to thank Lois Duke-Whitaker, Craig Brians, Kyle Saunders, Andrew Seligsohn, and Zoe Oxley. We are also grateful to many additional political scientists, too numerous to mention, who provided valuable feedback and insight on our conference papers and journal manuscripts related to this project. The anonymous reviewers, including those for this book, proved especially valuable.

At Hartwick College several students served as excellent research assistants on this project including Jennifer Bezanson '07,

Jennifer Lonergan '09, and Caitlin Hill '09. Laurel's father Richard Elder also edited and gave sage advice on several chapters of the book for which we are very grateful. The members of the Political Science Department at Hartwick, both past and present, have not only been wonderful colleagues, but have always been supportive of this research. We are grateful to Hartwick College for providing support for this project, including a Faculty Research Grant. At North Carolina State, members of the School of Public and International Affairs, especially Mike Cobb, Richard Clerkin, Bill Boettcher, Michael Struett, and Charlie Coe were always ready with feedback and support. Two NCSU undergraduates, Mark Yacoub '09 and Elizabeth Ivey '08, were instrumental in our work on chapter four.

Of course, we could not have done this without the help and support of our families and our friends. Laurel is especially grateful for the patience and love of her husband Mike, her daughter Indigo, and her poodle Henry who sat on her lap throughout most of the writing of this book. Laurel would also like to thank Steve who always believed they could finish and publish this book, even when she was not so sure. Steve went from a father of one to a father of four during the course of this project and could not have done it without the support and advice of his wife Kim. It is obligatory to thank your family for all the time away while you were working on the book. In this case, that's not necessary, which is why this book took so long. He would be remiss, though, not to acknowledge the four who make this title especially relevant to him and so slowed his progress: David, Alex, Evan, and Sarah.

At SUNY Press we would especially like to thank Michael Rinella who always believed in this project and stuck with us longer than we deserved. The rest of SUNY Press has been a model of professionalism in bringing this book to press.

Finally, we wish to thank our parents, to whom we dedicate this book, for love and support and encouraging our own love of politics.

1

Parenthood Is Political

This book is an exploration into how parenthood and the family have become politicized in American politics. Despite the centrality of raising children in the lives of many voters, and despite the emergence and prominence of topics concerning parents and the family within the national political debate, parenthood has not been a central focus in political science scholarship. There are very few acts more personal and intense in life than raising children. In this book we show how this very personal and intense act of raising a family is a politically defining experience and has come front and center into the political debate.

The central argument of this book is that parenthood is political. The transition to parenthood introduces dramatic and long-term changes into the lives of adults. Becoming a parent and raising children are significant adult socialization experiences, which, like getting married, entering the workforce, or growing older, hold the potential to shape political priorities, attitudes, and behavior. Over the last half century, the social and political environment surrounding America's families has changed in ways that have intensified the parenting experience and the importance of the family in national political debates.

The structure of the American family changed dramatically since the 1950s. Traditional nuclear families, in which fathers take on the role of economic provider while mothers care for the home and the children, are no longer the dominant family structure. The number of single-parent families has increased, and they now represent about one-third of all households with children.

1

Additionally, parents of both sexes are working longer hours to support their families and cover the costs associated with raising children. This is especially true for mothers, the majority of whom, whether unmarried or married, are now seeking to balance work outside the home with their continued roles as the primary caregivers for their children.

Despite these increased work hours and the demands of contemporary life, surveys reveal that parents place high value on their parental roles and identities, and detailed time diaries document that parents are spending as much and in many cases more time with their children than their parents and grandparents did (Bianchi, Robinson, and Milkie 2006). Given these changes, it is not surprising to find that parents today report higher levels of stress than other groups in society (Bianchi, Robinson, and Milkie 2006).

In response to these changes in the American family, there has been a dramatic politicization of parenthood by the major parties and the news media. As we document in this book, in the 1950s and 1960s, when the traditional father-breadwinner, mother-homemaker family was the norm, the topics of family and raising children were not part of mainstream political discourse. Presidents and presidential candidates did not discuss the importance of the family as an institution in American society in their public addresses, nor did they make explicit appeals to parents. Over the last four decades there has been a remarkable change in the content and tone of American politics and campaigns as they relate to parenthood and the family.

Starting in the 1980s and increasing dramatically across the 1990s, the political parties and their presidential candidates have tried to outdo one another in appealing directly to parents and in portraying themselves as the true champions of the American family. In his 1988 State of the Union address, Republican president Ronald Reagan pledged that his administration would "make certain that the family is always at the center of the public policy process." The Democrats soon followed. In his 1996 State of the Union address, President Bill Clinton stated that "Family is the foundation of American life. If we have stronger families, we will have a stronger America."

This emphasis on parenthood and the family has continued into the twenty-first century. During the buildup to the 2004 presidential election, both major party candidates and their wives made time to sit down with popular daytime television talk show hosts to talk about raising families (Sweet 2004a). Both parties also spoke explicitly to the concerns of "Security Moms" worried about the safety of their families, and "NASCAR Dads" anxious about the economic and moral health of the nation. In 2008, parents were, once again, given a high-profile role in the presidential campaign. The Republican ticket frequently drew on vice presidential candidate Sarah Palin's status as a mother and self-identified "Hockey Mom" to underscore the party's commitment to economic and social policies that would strengthen the family. The Democrats identified "Empowering America's Families for a New Era" as the lead issue in their 2008 platform and used the language of the family to frame their entire domestic agenda from energy to economics. Simply put, parenthood and the family have moved from the margins to the mainstream of partisan politics and political discourse.

The increased focus on parenthood and the family has been born out of electoral necessity and strategy. As the landscape of American families changed, the parties seized the opportunity to exploit social group divisions that were not previously relevant to politics, such as stressed-out parents and segments of the electorate deeply concerned about the decline of the traditional family (Arnold and Weisberg 1996, 194). Both parties realized that parent appeals make strategic sense. Not only do parents form a significant minority of voters, about 40 percent of the electorate in recent elections, but parenthood and family themes resonate across a range of economic, racial, and geographic divisions.

While both parties have politicized parenthood and the family, their messages about what pro-family and pro-parent policies should look like are quite different. Over the decades, the Republican Party has increasingly wrapped parent-family frames around their proposals for tax cuts and smaller government. In 2008, the Republican platform declared that making tax cuts permanent was vital to helping families survive the economic downturn. The party has also promoted a wide array of social policies as ways to strengthen parental rights and help parents protect their children from illicit societal influences.

In contrast, Democrats appealed to American parents by pledging more government regulation (e.g., mandating family leave policies, raising the minimum wage, implementing more environmental regulations, supporting a more generous social safety net) and endorsing policies supporting a broader array of lifestyle choices and family arrangements. In their 2008 platform, Democrats argued that increased government action to provide universal health care, ensure Americans get good jobs with good pay, preserve social security, and combat poverty was the best way to help America's working parents through economically challenging times. Scholars have documented the polarization of the parties over issues including abortion and women's rights (Adams 1997; Wolbrecht 2000). We argue that these growing divides are part of the politicization of the American family, a broader trend in American politics.

Elected officials, candidates, and the national parties were not alone in politicizing parenthood. As we empirically document in this book, they were joined in this development by the news media. Parenthood and the family first emerged as an identifiable theme in election coverage in 1980, but did not become a dominant theme until the 1992 presidential election. That is the year the Republican Party held a "Family Values" night during their national convention and Vice President Dan Quayle criticized the fictional television character Murphy Brown for mocking the importance of fathers in raising children. In every election since 1992, the news media have relied heavily on parents and the family as central frames in their coverage. Parent-based political labels such as "Soccer Moms," "NASCAR Dads," and "Security Moms" have become a predictable feature of each election cycle. They are now household phrases used by average citizens in discussing politics and elections. Reflecting the electoral environment of the 2008 election, new parent-based labels, including "Mortgage Moms" and "Walmart Moms," were employed by the news media as a way of discussing the parties' contrasting domestic agendas.

The media's politicization of parenthood is in part a reflection of political reality, the increasingly family-friendly language and policies offered by the political parties. Additionally, the news media have politicized parenthood because of the journalistic value of stories about "NASCAR Dads" or "Walmart Moms." Stories about how each party's proposals may or may not help struggling moms and dads are enticing to readers, quick and inexpensive to report, and provide an attractive way to discuss the issue positions of the candidates and frame the significance of poll results. Finally, the politicization of parenthood has been driven by the increasing number of news stories portraying parents as swing voters who have the power to determine the outcome of elections. Some news commentators have argued that the most significant divide in the American electorate is no longer the red state–blue state divide but a "baby gap," a divide between parents and non-parents (see Brooks 2004; Kotkin and Frey 2004; Sailer 2004). In a *New York Times* editorial titled "The New Red-Diaper Babies," David Brooks argued that there is a significant group of people in the United States for whom "personal identity is defined by parenthood" and that these people make their political decisions based on what will best protect their children. In the minds of the media, parenthood has joined the ranks of race, gender, class, and geography in becoming a highly significant political force.

At the center of these converging trends are parents themselves. They perceive their job of raising children to be harder than ever and more important than ever, and they are deeply concerned about providing for and protecting their children. One of the central questions we address in this book is how these changes in political rhetoric and media coverage have been reflected in the politics of America's parents and whether parents truly are the distinctive political bloc assumed by the parties and the news media. Most of the social science literature concerning parents and families has focused on how parents and the family environment shape the political leanings of children, but very few studies have looked at the reverse—the impact of having and raising children on the political beliefs and voting behavior of parents.

In a *Reader's Digest* article on "The Family Gap," Fred Barnes stated, "You think differently when you have kids" (1992, 50). In this book we provide compelling evidence, and the first systematic empirical data, that parents do "think differently" when it comes to politics. Our analyses show that parents are distinctive from their peers without children in terms of their political attitudes on many important issues. The fact that parents have greater concern for issues directly related to raising children such as funding for education may not be surprising. Nevertheless, this is one of the first studies to empirically document this basic parenthood effect.

More surprising is that parenthood has effects on issues beyond those directly or intimately connected to children including a general orientation toward the role of government.

The ideological directions of parenthood effects are not always consistent with the media's portrayal and conventional wisdom about parents. Rather than finding parents to be a distinctively conservative group, our results support the idea advanced by many feminist thinkers that time spent raising children has liberalizing political effects. Moreover, on several key issues parenthood pushes women and men in opposite ideological directions. All together these findings add richness to our understanding of political socialization throughout the life cycle and provide a more complete understanding of the causes of the gender gap.

Research Approach and Data

This book offers a comprehensive, objective, and empirically rigorous analysis of how and why parenthood has become politicized over the last half century, and what this means for American elections and politics. Most books concerning politics and the family are normative or prescriptive analyses reflecting the starkly different reactions to the changes in American families over the past fifty years. These books argue over what a true pro-family policy agenda entails, what elected officials should do to better support America's families, and the best way for parents to structure their lives. This book takes a very different approach, relying on multiple empirical methods to present an objective analysis of the politicization and polarization of parenthood and the family in American politics.

To document the politicization of parenthood and the family in elite political discourse and within the news media, we rely on rigorous content analyses of party documents including presidential speeches and party platforms, and print news media from 1952 to the present. Extending back to 1952 allows us to track changes in the use of "family language" before, during, and after the significant changes to the family. We also provide a detailed contextual analysis of these documents, so as to identify not just how much the political parties, presidential candidates, and major news media are talking about parent and family themes, but what they are saying. Multivariate analyses are employed to show that the increased references to parents and the family are statistically as well as substantively significant.

To explore the political attitudes and voting behavior of parents, we rely on two long-standing data sets, the American National Election Studies, which goes back to 1952, and the General Social Survey, which goes back to 1972. These two well-established data sets allow us to track the political attitudes of parents versus non-parents as the family and the political environment have undergone significant changes. While these two data sets have some overlap, each also contains unique measures of several important concepts not contained in its counterpart. Using both data sets allows us to examine the effects of parenthood on a wide range of important issues and provides greater analytical power. Additionally, these data sets contain a rich array of demographic and socioeconomic variables, which allows us to employ multivariate models controlling for potentially confounding variables so that we can better isolate and explore the impact of parenthood.

Overview of the Book

The next chapter of this book, chapter 2, highlights the major changes to the American family over the past half century, with particular emphasis on how these changes are politically relevant. The chapter draws on recent U.S. Census data, as well as the latest research of demographers, family studies experts, and sociologists to document and interpret changes in the structure of American families. This chapter also explores the important interaction between gender and parenthood. Despite major changes to the American family, parenting continues to be a highly gendered activity both in terms of societal attitudes about the appropriate roles of mothers and fathers and in terms of the actual roles and responsibilities male and female parents take on. Female parents are expected to and continue to play a much larger and more nurturing role in the parenting process than their male counterparts, a reality that has multiple political consequences. Thus, while this is a book about the politicization of parents, a major theme is that men and women are affected by parenthood in very different ways.

Chapter 3 shows that parenthood and the family have gone from being essentially non-political and non-partisan issues—

rarely being mentioned in platforms, speeches, and presidential campaigns—to providing a fundamental frame for the broad domestic policy agendas of both parties, and providing the basis for new policy initiatives explicitly directed toward parents. We argue that the politicization of parenthood has been driven by strategic political parties and candidates seeking an advantage in the new political environment created by the dramatic changes in the American family discussed in chapter 2. In contemporary politics, American parents find themselves sought after by both parties, who promise to strengthen their families and empower them to better protect their children. The politicization of parenthood and the family by the parties and their standard-bearers not only reveals much about party behavior and issue evolution, but is significant given the demonstrated potential of issue frames to influence how voters think and act politically.

Chapter 4 documents that the news media have politicized parenthood and the family in three important ways. First, the print news media have increasingly relied on parenthood and the family as a way of making sense of election events and as a means of communicating what they believe is at stake in policy disputes and election outcomes. Secondly, the media have increasingly used parents and families as a lens through which to discuss a wide range of issues, including the most pertinent and pressing issues during each electoral cycle. Finally, the media have increasingly portrayed parents as pivotal swing voters, which heightens their attractiveness as targets for politicians. The increasing media usage of parent-family frames reinforces and is reinforced by political actors, but also serves the increased commercialization of news values.

Responding to all the changing pressures of parenthood and the increased discussion of parenthood and the family in political discourse has been the parents themselves. Chapters 5 and 6 look at the effects of parenthood on the political attitudes of mothers and fathers. Chapter 5 provides overtime analysis of the politics of parents—their political attitudes on major policy issues as well as their partisanship, ideology, and vote choice. Given that parenting remains a very different experience for male and female parents, we break down all of our results by sex. We find that parenthood is indeed political. Men and women with children in the home are significantly different than their counterparts without children on a wide range of issues, not just on issues directly related to childrearing.

Additionally we find that parenthood affects women and men differently. Women are more affected by parenthood than men, not surprising given their much greater role in parenting. On the majority of issues parenthood is associated with ideologically opposing effects for women and men. Motherhood is associated with more liberal attitudes, whereas fatherhood is associated with more conservative attitudes. The issue domains where parenthood effects are strongest vary by gender as well. These results are significant in not only providing insights into the political impact of parenthood as an agent of political socialization, but in providing some of the first empirical evidence that parenthood contributes to the gender gap on political issues, vote choice, and partisanship.

In chapter 6 we delve more deeply into the effect of parenthood on political attitudes. By employing multivariate regression models we explore whether the motherhood and fatherhood effects documented in the previous chapter remain significant predictors of political attitudes on major policy issues as well as broader political orientations when potentially confounding factors such as age, income, education, and religion are controlled. We also deepen our understanding of the political impact of parenthood by taking a more extensive look at the relationship between parenthood and two potentially mediating variables: the marital status and the race/ethnicity of parents. We find that not only do parenthood effects remain in multivariate models, but parenthood appears to politicize the politics of men and women in similar ways regardless of race. We also find that for men parenthood and marriage act as reinforcing pressures both pushing attitudes in a conservative direction, but for women parenthood and marriage act as cross-pressures. Motherhood is associated with liberal effects while marriage is associated with conservative effects.

Chapter 7, our concluding chapter, takes a broader look at both the theoretical and practical significance of the empirical findings presented in the book. In this chapter we take a step back to examine what the politics of parenthood teaches us about public opinion, political socialization across the life cycle, and the gender gap. We also look to the future of parenthood and family politics given demographic trends and the evolving national agenda. Moreover, we argue that the way parenthood and the family have been politicized in the U.S. political system is not neutral in its impacts. Rather it highlights and advantages some types of parents, while marginalizing the concerns of other groups in society including women, poor families, and single parents. We conclude by laying out several avenues for further research on the politics of parenthood.

2

The Politics of the Changing American Family

Having and raising children has always brought about profound, long-term change in the lives of adults. Over the last several decades, the societal context in which parenting takes place has changed in ways that have increased concerns about the family as well as the challenges and pressures that parents face. The American family has changed dramatically. Traditional nuclear families are no longer the dominant type of household. Those who have children are working more hours outside of the home than ever before. This is especially true for mothers who have dramatically increased their participation in the paid workforce over the past several decades.

Despite these significant changes, there are also areas of striking continuity in American families over the last half century. Women and men continue to play distinct roles in the parenting process reflecting traditional conceptions of the roles of mothers and fathers. Americans continue to value family life very highly, and parents find their children the most fulfilling aspect of their lives. Despite increased work hours and the busyness of contemporary life, parents in the twenty-first century are spending as much or more time with their children than their own parents or grandparents did with their children. In this chapter we review the major changes and areas of continuity within the American family, and more importantly, outline their political consequences.

The Changing American Family

One of the most discussed changes in American family life has been the decline of the traditional nuclear family. In the 1950s, the traditional father-breadwinner, mother-homemaker family was the dominant structure of family life in the United States (Coontz 1992). Over the next half century, such traditionally structured families became less and less common. In 1970, married couple households with children formed 40 percent of all households. Four decades later, in 2010, married couples with children formed only 21 percent of all the households in the United States (see table 2.1).

One reason for the decline in traditionally structured households is that marriage has become a much less common experi-

Table 2.1. The Changing Context of Parenting in the United States

	1955	1970s	1980	1990	2000	2010
Married couples with children as a percentage of all households in the U.S.	N/A	40	31	26	26	21
Percent of families with children headed by single parent	N/A	13	22	28	31	32
Percent of mothers with children under 18 in the workforce	27	47.4	57	67	73	71
Percent of mothers with children under 6 in the workforce	18	39	47	58	65	64

Source for Household-Family data is U.S. Census Bureau. Data for 1970s column is from 1970 for first two rows and 1975 for last two rows. Working Mothers data are from U.S. Bureau of Labor Statistics, and data in last column are actually for 2008.

ence in American society. In the 1950s, married couples dominated the social landscape of the United States, forming about 80 percent of all households. By 1970 this figure had dropped to 71 percent and by 2005 slightly less than 50 percent of households were composed of married couples (Roberts 2007). Declining marriage rates are the product of several forces: more people are delaying marriage until later in life, an increasing number of couples are living together without getting married, and divorce rates have increased, especially across the 1970s and 1980s (Coontz 2005; Fields 2004; Pew Research Center 2010).

A related change, and one more central to the emphasis of this book, has been the growing disconnect between parenting and marriage. While most parents today are married—the proportion of families with children that are headed by married parents leveled off during the mid-1990s at about 68 percent—marriage and childrearing have become increasingly disconnected. In 1970, 12 percent of families with children were headed by a single mother and 1 percent of families with children were headed by a single father (table 2.1). According to recent census data, single parents now form about 32 percent of families with children, with 27 percent of families with children headed by a single mother and 5 percent headed by a single father.

Parents are also a smaller portion of the population today than they were fifty years ago. In 1976 about 10 percent of women nearing the end of their child-bearing years did not have children. By 2008 this figure had increased to 18 percent (Dye 2010). Additionally, Americans are having fewer children. In the baby boom of the late 1950s, women were having an average of 3.5 children, and by 2008, this had dropped down to an average of 1.9 children per woman (Dye 2010).

In addition to the decline of the nuclear family, the other "revolution" in American family life has been the influx of mothers into the workforce. In the 1950s a majority of women were not in the paid workforce. This was especially true for married women and mothers. In the 1950s about 27 percent of mothers overall, and 18 percent of mothers with children under six, worked outside the home. As of 2008 the percent of mothers in the paid workforce had increased to 71 percent (table 2.1). Even the majority of women with very young children, about 62 percent, now participate in the paid labor force. In fact, women with children under six were the fastest growing segment of the labor force across the 1990s (Anderson and Vail 1999, 360). Despite recent news stories about "the opt-out mom," the number of mothers who work outside the home continues to remain steady and high.[1]

Any study on parenthood and politics in the twenty-first century must take note of some significant differences among racial and ethnic groups in terms of parenthood and family arrangements. The decreasing rates of marriage discussed previously are particularly pronounced among non-whites. According to 2009 Census data, only 31 percent of African Americans are married and living with their spouse compared to 47 percent of Hispanics and 54 percent of white Americans. Additionally, the disconnect between marriage and children is particularly pronounced among African Americans. A majority of African American families with children are headed by single mothers, while white and Asian American families with children are more likely to be led by married parents. In 2004, 62 percent of births to African American women were non-marital as compared to 32 percent for Hispanic women and 25 percent for whites (Dye 2005, 5). Finally, a greater percentage of Hispanic women are having children than African Americans or whites. In 2004, 22 percent of births in the United States were to Hispanic mothers, which is higher than Hispanics' overall representation in American society at about 14 percent (Dye 2005).

Finally, a considerable number of parents today are struggling economically (Dye 2010). Economist Edward Wolff traced the economic status of parents from the 1960s into the beginning of the twenty-first century and demonstrated that poverty rates among families with children have always been higher than those without children (2002, 59). Over the last four decades, however, the gap in poverty rates between families with and without children has widened, a trend that holds for both married and unmarried parents (Wolff 2002, 61). In part this is due to stagnating wages, but it is also a product of the socioeconomic status of those becoming parents. Census data show that birth rates have been dropping and are now below the national average among the highly educated and the wealthy. Meanwhile married and unmarried women with low family incomes were more likely to have children than women in higher income groups (Dye 2010, 2005). Another indicator of the economic struggles of parents is that, as of 2001, close to one-fifth of mothers (19 percent) were participants in one or more government assistance programs.[2] This figure is even higher, 25 percent, among women with infants, and extremely high among minority parents with newborns (Dye 2010). A majority, 56 percent, of African American mothers with infants were participants in government assistance programs as compared to 43 percent of Hispanic mothers and 21 percent of white mothers (Lugaila 2005). While raising children is a costly endeavor for all parents, the economic struggles of single parents are especially pronounced. A third of families headed by single mothers have incomes below the poverty level (Fields 2004, 9).

The changes to the American family outlined thus far have several politically significant consequences. First, parenting has become a less common and less homogenous experience among the American public. In terms of their percentage of the population, parents are a smaller electoral bloc today than they were in the 1950s. As we will discuss more in the following chapters, it is ironic, but perhaps not altogether surprising, that the political parties, presidential candidates, and the news media have given parents increasing attention in their campaigns and election coverage over the same time period that an increasing percentage of American adults have been delaying marriage and choosing to not become parents.

Secondly, parents are raising children in different family contexts than in the past. A majority of mothers are in the workforce and a third of families with children are headed by single parents. One of the consequences of these dramatic changes has been a resurgence of concern over the American family and what many view as its decline. Organizations including the Moral Majority and the Christian Coalition emerged in response to these changes in the American family and focused their political energies on restoring the traditional nuclear family. Historians and family studies scholars have shown that "the family in crisis," the "embattled family," and the need for social reforms to "protect the family" have been recurring themes in American society since before the Civil War and throughout the twentieth century (Ribuffo 2006; Skolnick 1991). What was new about the emergence of these

organizations starting in the late 1970s was their embrace of explicitly political strategies, including efforts to shape party platforms
and electoral outcomes, and explicit efforts to shape the political
and policy agenda.

Another political consequence of these changes has been the
increased reliance of parents on government programs and those
outside the immediate family for help in caring for their families.
For the third of parents who are raising children without a spouse,
and for the majority of families where the mother is working outside the home, it is increasingly necessary to rely on people and
programs—including day care, universal pre-K, and after school
programs—outside of the traditional family to provide much of
their children's care (Anderson and Vail 1999). As discussed, for
a growing and sizable minority of adults, becoming a parent has
pushed them into poverty and direct reliance on government
assistance programs from Medicaid to housing assistance to food
assistance programs. Thus, parenthood is increasingly associated
with use of and reliance on a wide range of government programs.

The Persistence of Gendered Parenting
Roles and Realities

Overtime studies of public opinion as well as detailed diaries
documenting how Americans spend their time have revealed both
continuity and change in Americans' attitudes about parenthood
and family life as well as the actual ways parenting is carried out.
Given the dramatic changes in the lives of parents over the last
century, it is somewhat surprising that gendered ideas about the
appropriate roles of mothers and fathers are still held by many
Americans, and that female and male parents continue to take on
very different roles in the childrearing process that are consistent
with these gendered expectations (Bianchi, Robinson, and Milkie
2006; Douglas and Michaels 2004).

The idea that mothers are supposed take care of the home and
be all-giving and nurturing to their children and to their families
has long been a cultural touchstone in American society (Rindfuss,
Brewster, and Kavee 1996; Risman 1998). Despite significant shifts
in public opinion over the last four decades to a place where a

majority of Americans now endorse most dimensions of gender equality, there remains a strong current of support for a gendered division of labor when it comes to caring for the home, and especially when it comes to caring for children. As figure 2.1 shows, a substantial minority of Americans continue to believe that men should achieve outside the home while women take care of the home and family. Many Americans are also concerned about the effects of mothers' employment in the paid workforce, believing that family life suffers when mothers are employed. Turning again to figure 2.1 we see that a considerable minority of Americans believe that women should stay home if they have children, especially if the children are young. Hays (1996) has argued that the pressures on women to be "good mothers," to "be there" for their children, and to spend quality time with their children have actually increased over recent decades.

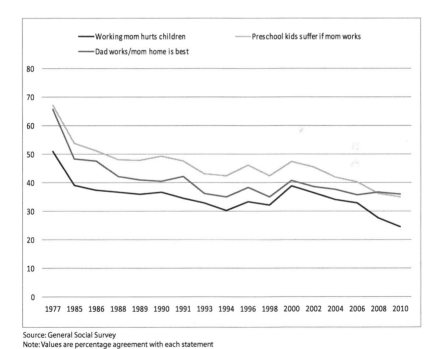

Source: General Social Survey
Note: Values are percentage agreement with each statement

Figure 2.1. Traditional Gender Role Attitudes in Recent Decades.

For men, it is still the case that being a good parent means working outside the home and providing economically for their families (Christiansen and Palkovitz 2001; Townsend 2002). Public opinion polls show strong support for the father-breadwinner role. A 2010 Pew Research survey indicated that some 67 percent of Americans say that in order to be ready for marriage, it is very important for a man to be able to support his family, while only 33 percent of respondents indicated that this was true for a woman (Pew Research Center 2010). In Nicholas Townsend's ethnographic study *The Package Deal* (2002), he found that fathers feel they can best demonstrate love and emotional closeness through providing economically for their families, as doing so allows their children to live in safe neighborhoods and gives their children the resources they need to be successful. At the same time there is now a slightly higher expectation that fathers will also spend more time with their children. Bianchi, Robinson, and Milkie's generational survey shows that men today are much more likely than past cohorts of men to believe that fathers should share in care-giving responsibilities, expectations also held by their wives and society more broadly (2006, 127).

As of the twenty-first century, mothers and fathers are, by and large, living up to these gendered expectations. Multiple studies have shown that men respond to fatherhood by increasing their hours at work (Burns, Schlozman, and Verba 2001, 311; Lunberg and Rose 2000, 2002; Nock 1998). Mothers still take on the majority of child care responsibilities and act as the primary nurturer and care-giver for their children (Bianchi, Robinson, and Milkie 2006; Elder and Greene 2008). Mothers are much more likely than fathers to stay out of the paid workforce to raise children full time (Fields 2004). Women's significantly greater involvement in raising children also exists in families where both parents work full time. The most recent data from the University of Wisconsin's National Survey of Families and Households show that when child care is defined as attending to the physical needs of a child, on average women do five times more child care than their husbands (Belkin 2008).

The political significance of these different roles and expectations for female and male parents is that fathers and mothers may respond differently to parenthood. Given mothers' attempts to balance work outside the home with primary care of their children, they may view government programs designed to provide services to families in a positive way. Women's greater role in nurturing children may also promote more pacifist views on military conflict and war. In contrast, given their responsibilities to provide economically for their families, fathers and husbands may have reason to embrace more conservative economic and social welfare policies. Although an expanded social welfare state may potentially ease the burden of their working wives, by providing more affordable child care or after school programs, men may view their paychecks as being whittled down by such policies (Iversen and Rosenbluth 2006).

Parental Identities and Commitment to Family

Studies show that despite declining rates of marriage, an increase in single parenting, and an exodus of mothers out of the home and into the workplace, Americans continue to value marriage, children, and family life as strongly as at any point in the past four decades. A recent Pew Research Center poll indicated that 76 percent of American adults say their family is the most important element of their life (Pew Research Center 2010). While more Americans see having children as a voluntary choice rather than something every married couple "should do," they also view parenthood as more important and fulfilling than ever. In their four-decade study of attitudes about the family, Thornton and Young-DeMarco found that "marriage and children are not only centrally significant and meaningful to the vast majority of Americans but may have become more valued, desired, and expected in recent decades" (2001, 1030). Moreover, evidence points to the idea that among mothers and fathers, being a parent is more important to their social identity. A 2007 survey by the Pew Research Center found that children are absolutely the center of parents' lives:

> Asked to weigh how important various aspects of their lives are to their personal happiness and fulfillment, parents in this survey place their relationships with their children on a pedestal rivaled only by their relationships with their spouses—and far above their relationships with their parents, friends, or their jobs or careers. This is true both for

married and unmarried parents. In fact, relatively speaking, children are most pre-eminent in the lives of unwed
parents. (4)

The increased importance parents place on their family life
and their relationships with their children may help explain a surprising trend uncovered by several different researchers. Despite
increased work hours, contemporary parents are managing to
spend as much or more time with their children than parents in
previous generations (Belkin 2008; Robinson and Godbey 1999;
Schor 2002, 91). Researchers examining maternal employment
and time with children have found that despite the dramatic influx
of mothers into the workforce, mothers are also spending as much
or more time with their children than in previous decades (Bianchi 2000). Using four decades of time diary data from parents,
Bianchi, Robinson, and Milkie (2006) document that although
maternal time with children did dip between 1965 and 1975, the
time today's mothers spend caring for their children is as high,
or higher, than during the 1960s—a trend which holds true for
both married and unmarried mothers. In 1965 mothers spent
10.2 hours a week tending primarily to their children. That figure is now higher than ever, at nearly 14.1 hours per week. While
there remains a sizable gender gap in parenting, studies show that
fathers have also increased the amount of focused time they spend
with their children and the number of child care tasks they take
on (Bianchi, Robinson, and Milkie 2006, 3 and 171). Interestingly,
although parent-child time has remained steady or increased over
the years, about half or more of American parents continue to feel
they spend too little time with their children (Bianchi, Robinson,
and Milkie 2006, 133; Schor 2002, 96).

The picture that emerges from these detailed, multiple decade
time diaries as well as overtime survey data is that being a parent
is an even higher priority in the lives of mothers and fathers today
than in past decades. Bianchi, Robinson, and Milkie conclude that
mothers are able to pull off this feat of increased work hours outside the home with increased quality time with their children "by
making children their top priority" (2006, 169). The researchers
also note, however, that this feat comes at a significant psychological cost to mothers who report "always feeling rushed," "not

having enough time for their spouse and for themselves," and often "juggling more than one thing at a time" (Bianchi, Robinson, and Milkie 2006, 169). Other researchers examining time diaries and perceptions of time report that mothers rate especially high on the "time crunch scale" (Robinson and Godbey 1999, 237). The stress and sense of time crunch associated with parenting is particularly intense for single parents (Bianchi, Robinson, and Milkie 2006, 173). While the stress of parenthood is particularly intense for mothers, fathers also report having less free time and higher levels of stress than their non-parent counterparts and are more likely to report that they always feel rushed (Robinson and Godbey 1999).

The evidence suggests that parenthood is a more important identity and role in the lives of adults today than in the past. Parents are managing to carve out as much or more quality time to spend with their children even while working more hours and balancing all their other responsibilities. Parents find their children the most fulfilling aspect of their lives and make their children a top priority in their lives. Parents are also more stressed than ever. We argue that all these forces combine to make the topic of parenthood, as well as parents themselves, particularly open to politicization in contemporary American politics.

3

"Family Values" vs. "Champion of Working Families"

Parenthood, Families, and the Political Parties

But let us make certain that the family is always at the center of the public policy process, not just in this administration but in all future administrations.

—President Ronald Reagan, 1988 State of Union address

Family is the foundation of American life. If we have stronger families, we will have a stronger America.

—President Bill Clinton, 1996 State of the Union address

In their analysis of issue evolution, Edward G. Carmines and James A. Stimson argue that "exogenous shocks to the system," or major societal changes, present new opportunities for strategic politicians and can spur partisan evolution on particular issues (1989, 4). Political parties, they argue, come to focus on certain issues or themes, such as race, not because they are fundamental to the political or electoral system, but because they "are well fitted into new niches provided by an evolving political environment" (1989, 4). In this chapter, we argue that the seismic changes in the structure of the family and parenting experience, documented in the previous chapter, acted as profound exogenous shocks to the political system. Over the last half century, the institutions of marriage and parenthood have become increasingly disconnected and the majority of mothers have moved from working primarily in the home to balancing their roles as primary care-givers of their children with work outside the home. Moreover, despite increased work hours, parents are spending more time with their children and value their role as parents more strongly than ever.

Out of these shocks to American society have emerged what Carmines and Stimson refer to as "unsatisfied constituencies" including parents stressed by efforts to combine family life with increasing work hours, mothers and fathers struggling to afford the increasing costs of raising children, and those increasingly concerned about the decline of the traditional family—groups that represented new opportunities for strategic parties interested in broadening their electoral coalitions. The central argument of this chapter is that the parties have responded to this evolving environment by strategically embracing themes of parenthood and the family. Over the past several decades the parties have reframed their core values with pro-family rhetoric and adopted a new set of social and cultural positions aimed to appeal directly to parents.

To assess how much, and perhaps more importantly, how the major parties talked about parenthood and the family from 1952 to the present, this chapter presents a quantitative and then a qualitative analysis of four types of documents: Republican and Democratic party platforms as well as transcripts of presidential State of the Union addresses,[1] inaugural addresses, and convention speeches made by the presidential nominees. These materials are good reflections of party beliefs, policy goals, and strategic appeals (Walters 1990, 438; Monroe 1983; Pomper 1980) and have been offered on a consistent basis over the past half century, making them well suited for meaningful comparisons over time and across parties. While other scholarship has examined the attention of the parties to family themes in specific elections, the analysis provided in this chapter is the first showing how the themes of family and parenthood evolved in the party system as the two major parties responded to the dramatic changes in the American family.

Quantitative Analysis of Parent-Family Themes in Platforms and Major Speeches

This chapter turns first to the quantitative analysis of the four types of documents mentioned earlier: party platforms, as well as transcripts of presidential State of the Union addresses, inaugural addresses, and convention speeches made by the presidential nominees. Table 3.1 provides descriptive statistics of the documents analyzed in this chapter, which includes thirty party platforms, thirty nomination acceptance speeches, fifteen inaugural addresses, and sixty State of the Union addresses. The text of each document was coded for the number of times it used the following keywords: family/families, children/child/kids, daughter, son, parent/parents/parenting, mother/mom, and father/dad. We often refer to these references collectively as "parent-family" references.

Figures 3.1 through 3.5 illustrate the results of this quantitative analysis and taken together show a clear, consistent, and dramatic picture of the politicization of parenthood and the family over the second half of the twenty-first century. The parties, their candidates, and their presidents have ratcheted up their references to parents, families, and children in their platforms and in their appeals to the American electorate across each decade, peaking in the last decade of the twentieth century. In addition to the graphs, table 3.2 presents multivariate analyses regressing parent-family reference totals on year and party in order to demonstrate the statistical significance of the trends in the graphs. The regression

Table 3.1. Descriptive Statistics of Parent-Family References by Document Type, 1952–2009

	Number	Minimum	Maximum	Mean	Std Dev
Platform	30	0	267	103.70	79.39
Inaugural	15	0	14	5.33	4.55
State of Union	60	1	106	21.52	23.26
Convention	30	2	114	25.03	226.13

Source: Author coding of political party platforms, nominating convention speeches, presidential inaugural addresses, and State of the Union addresses

Table 3.2. OLS Regression of Parent-Family Mentions by Year and Party, 1952–2009

	Platform	Inaugural	State of Union	Convention
Constant	−35.28	2.99	20.988*	11.88
	(29.49)	(3.67)	(8.14)	(11.52)
Year	3.70**	.151*	.87**	1.07**
	(.48)	(.053)	(.13)	(.19)
Party	23.53	−1.26	−14.7**	−11.27*
	(16.60)	(1.88)	(4.48)	(6.49)
Adjusted R^2	.67	.34	.47	.54
N	30	15	60	30

**$p \leq .01$; *$p \leq .05$, two-tailed tests

Source: Author coding of political party platforms, nominating convention speeches, presidential inaugural addresses, and State of the Union addresses.

Note: Year indicates years from 1952, which is coded as 0. Party is coded 1 for Republican and 0 for Democrat.

models strongly confirm that the relationship between time and parent-family references is quite significant, both statistically and substantively, for each type of document.[2]

We turn now to a more detailed discussion of the party platforms illustrated in figures 3.1 and 3.2. Figure 3.1 shows that in the first year of our analysis, 1952, the combined number of Republican and Democratic references to parent-family terms was twenty-seven. By 1992 this figure had surpassed the 300 mark, and in 2000 it reached its absolute high of 407. Since party platforms vary in length across parties and across time, a standardized version of the platform analysis, controlling for the number of words in each platform, is presented in figure 3.2. When controlling for length, the overall trend is very similar, although the high point in combined parent-family references was reached in 1992.

The platform analysis also reveals that the politicization of the family has been a bipartisan phenomenon. Despite conventional wisdom that the Republican Party has been the party of "family values" and thus the driver of the political debate over the family,

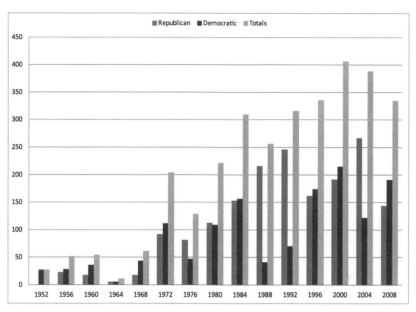

Figure 3.1. Party Platforms. Total Parent-Family References.

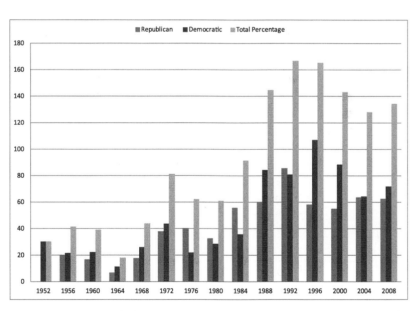

Figure 3.2. Party Platforms. Parent-Family References Controlling for Platform Length.

there is rough parity between the two parties in employing family-friendly rhetoric. Figure 3.2, which tracks each party's parent-family references while controlling for the number of words in the platforms, shows that the extent to which the parties make use of family-friendly rhetoric is remarkably similar over time. Meanwhile, figure 3.1, which shows the raw number of parent-family references in platforms over time, shows a Republican advantage in 1988, 1992, and 2004, but a Democratic advantage in 1996, 2000, and 2008. Although not shown, when broken down by specific parent-family terms, 2008 represents an all-time high for Democrats' use of the terms "family" and "father." The 2008 election also represents the first time in over three decades that the Democrats included more references to "families" in their platform than Republicans (77 to 68). Despite Republican vice presidential candidate Sarah Palin's frequent use of the term "Hockey Mom" in her communications with the public, the 2008 Republican platform only contained one reference to "mothers/moms," compared to five for the 2008 Democratic platform.

Figure 3.3 illustrates the use of parent-family terms in presidential nomination acceptance speeches from 1952 to 2008. This figure shows that the presidential nominees have increasingly utilized family themes in making their cases to the American public. Mirroring the platforms, the absolute high in parent-family references was reached in 2000 when Al Gore and George W. Bush collectively made 152 family-parent references when accepting their parties' presidential nominations. While the speeches of Democrat Barack Obama and Republican John McCain in 2008 did not come close to reaching those in 2000, the 2008 figures remain higher in absolute and relative terms than the decades prior to the 1980s, and the regression models included in table 3.2 show that the increase over time remains statistically significant.

The analysis of presidential nomination speeches shown in figure 3.3 also reinforces the finding that the politicization of parenthood and the family has been a bipartisan phenomenon. While the party conventions of 1992 might be best remembered for the Republican Party's "Family Values Night" and vice presidential candidate Dan Quayle's Murphy Brown "family values" speech (Arnold and Weisberg 1996), this is the year when Democratic presidential nominees began to outpace their Republican

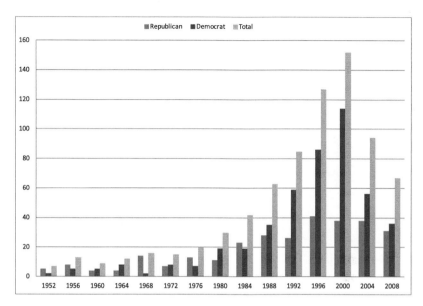

Figure 3.3. Convention Speeches. Parent-Family References.

counterparts in talking about parents and the family. In 1996 and 2000, Bill Clinton and Al Gore respectively made parents, kids, and family central themes in their convention addresses by working 86 and 114 parent-family references into their speeches, significantly more than their Republican counterparts. Although by a smaller margin, Democratic presidential nominees John Kerry and Barack Obama also incorporated more references to parent and family themes in their acceptance speeches than their Republican counterparts. Table 3.2 indicates that the Democratic advantage in the use of parent-family language in convention speeches is statistically significant in regression analysis.

Analysis of the fifty-two State of the Union addresses (figure 3.4) also shows that presidents of both parties drove the politicization of parenthood and the family. Two time periods in our study are characterized by a significant stepping up in family-rhetoric, the 1980s during the presidency of Ronald Reagan, and the 1990s during the presidency of Bill Clinton. Similar to the platforms and convention speeches, the parent-family highpoint in State of Union addresses is reached in 2000, the final address of Bill Clinton, in

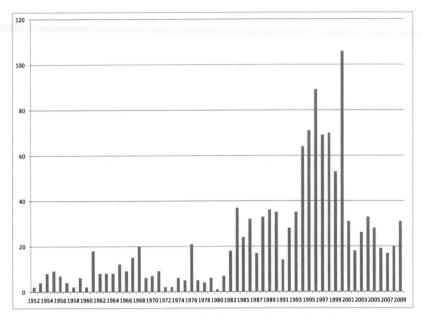

Figure 3.4. State of the Union Addresses. Parent-Family References, 1952–2009.

which he made 106 parent-family references. While the increased usage of parent-family terms over time is statistically significant (table 3.2), it is important to note that President Obama's invocation of parent-family themes represents a drop from the speeches of President Clinton. As with the convention addresses, table 3.2 shows the Democratic advantage remains statistically significant in regression analysis.

Inaugural addresses are much shorter than the other documents examined and as a result contain far fewer parent-family references: There were on average fewer than six in each address (table 3.1). Although there are some decreases, figure 3.5 shows a general pattern of increasing parent-family rhetoric throughout the 1980s and 1990s, and this trend is statistically significant as shown in table 3.2. One of the most pronounced drops in parent-family references took place between President George W. Bush's first and second inaugural addresses (figure 3.5). This decline reflects a shift in national focus, in the wake of the September 11, 2001 terrorist attacks, away from domestic issues to national defense

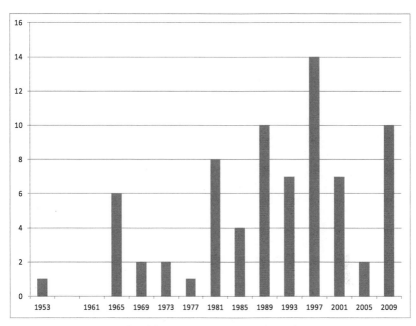

Figure 3.5. Inaugural Addresses. Parent-Family References, 1953–2009.

and international issues, a realm where parties are less likely to incorporate the language of the family. It is also important to note that President Obama's 2009 inaugural address is tied for second highest in terms of references to parents and families, surpassed only by President Clinton in 1997.

Taken as a whole, the quantitative results tell an unmistakable story of both parties increasingly using parent-family rhetoric in their communication with the American public. Across four divergent set of sources—convention speeches, State of the Union addresses, inaugural addresses, and party platforms—there were statistically and substantively significant increases in the usage of this rhetoric.

Qualitative Analysis of Family-Parent References

While the quantitative results are compelling, quantitative analysis alone cannot capture the content of the parties' discourse and pledges, which is essential for a full understanding of the politics of parenthood. This section presents the results of a contextual analysis of the substance of the references. For this qualitative analysis, we examined what issue or set of issues the parent-family references are used to frame; and, following the approach used by Sanbonmatsu (2004) and Cohen (1997) in their examinations of party evolution on other issues, we examine the policy direction of the references (whether the references can be categorized as liberal or conservative) and whether the parties take similar or opposing positions. This section makes sense of the thousands of parent-family references by highlighting the most significant changes in their policy content, ideological direction, and level of partisan similarity/difference over the last half century.

The 1950s and 1960s: Helping Families and Children in Need

Throughout the 1950s and 1960s, the parties' parent-family references are similar not only in their small number—as documented previously, parent-family references are at the low point during these two decades—but also in their policy content and ideological direction (see table 3.3). First, the parties are similar in what they did not say. In their platforms and speeches, neither party defined the family or referred to family values. Neither party offered general support for the family as an important institution in American society, nor discussed the need for any social policies designed to protect or strengthen the family. Neither party talked about, nor to, "parents"; this term was simply outside mainstream political rhetoric.[3] The small number of parent-family references focused primarily on a narrow set of issues: the concerns of low-income families, particularly the plight of farm families, and disadvantaged children. Thus, when parties and their candidates did use parent-family terms, they were not references to the family per se, but colloquial ways of referring to certain groups, such as farmers and low-income adults and children. Moreover, these references were decidedly not appeals to parents, but rather appeals to society as a whole about the need to help the less advantaged in society. In the coming decades, this bipartisan emphasis on low-income families is abandoned for rhetoric dealing almost exclusively with middle-class families.

Table 3.3. Partisan Language about the Family and Parenthood in the 1950s and 1960s

Republican Party	Democratic Party
The Republican Party pledges itself to develop new programs to improve and stabilize farm family income. —1960 Republican platform	Promote programs which will protect and preserve the family type farm as a bulwark of American life . . . including additional assistance to family farmers and young farmers. —1956 Democratic platform
As part of our efforts to provide decent, safe and sanitary housing for low-income families, we must carry forward the housing program authorized during the 83rd Congress. —Eisenhower, 1956 State of the Union	Twelve long years after Congress declared our goal to be "a decent home and a suitable environment for every American family," we still have 25 million Americans living in substandard homes. A new housing program under a new Housing and Urban Affairs Department will be needed this year. —Kennedy, 1961 State of the Union
We must aid in cushioning the heavy and rising costs of illness and hospitalization to individuals and families. —Eisenhower, 1955 State of the Union	The program I shall propose will emphasize this cooperative approach to help that one-fifth of all American families with incomes too small to even meet their basic needs. —Johnson, 1964 State of the Union
Other needs in the area of social welfare include increased child welfare services, extension of the program of aid to dependent children, intensified attack on juvenile delinquency, and special attention to the problems of mentally retarded children. —Eisenhower, 1956 State of the Union	The future of America depends on adequate provision by Government for the needs of those of our children who cannot be cared for by their parents or private social agencies. —1956 Democratic platform

continued on next page

Table 3.3. *Continued.*

Republican Party	Democratic Party
To treat the special problems of children from impoverished families, we advocate expanded, better programs for pre-school children. —1968 Republican platform	The new pre-school program known as Head Start has proven its effectiveness in widening the horizons of over two million poor children and their parents. —1968 Democratic platform

During these decades, the parties' few parent-family references are fairly similar in ideological direction. As summarized in table 3.3, both parties state that government needs to do more to help needy families and disadvantaged children, and both parties offer government programs and spending as solutions. Again and again in his State of the Union addresses, Republican president Dwight Eisenhower speaks of the need to help low-income families acquire adequate housing, aid in cushioning rising medical costs that put hardships on families, construct more public schools, increase child welfare services, extend the program of aid to dependent children, and better address the needs of children who are disadvantaged mentally, physically, and economically. During this same time, the Democrats similarly discuss the need to construct more low-income housing and public school facilities, to provide health centers to serve the needs of the poor, to improve social welfare programs assisting low-income families, and ensure child health and welfare services are maintained and extended. During these decades, the parties are quite similar in terms of the level of attention, policy content, and ideological direction of their parent-family references. The differences between the parties are more in terms of empha-sis. Although both parties advocate the need for government inter-vention on behalf of America's struggling families, the Democratic Party devotes relatively more platform space and stronger language to such themes, especially under President Johnson.

Republicans: Smaller Government Needed to Protect the Traditional Family

In the decades following the 1960s, the themes of parenthood and the family become increasingly integrated into elite rhetoric. Both parties begin to devote prominent space in their platforms and national addresses to recognizing the importance of the family per se as an institution in American society. For the Republicans, this begins in earnest under Ronald Reagan, who continually holds up the family as one of the nation's bedrock values, crucial to America's greatness. In his 1988 State of the Union address, Reagan pledged his administration would "make certain that the family is always at the center of the public policy process" and mandated every department and agency review its activities to make sure they were consistent with promoting the family. Exhortations such as these became a mainstay of Republican rhetoric. For example, in 1992 President George Bush affirmed "we must strengthen the family, because it is the family that has the greatest bearing on our future." Similarly, the 2004 Republican platform states, "The family is society's central core of energy. That is why efforts to strengthen family life are the surest way to improve life for everyone."

Platitudes about the greatness of the family, in and of themselves, are difficult to categorize ideologically. Starting in the 1980s, however, the ideological direction of Republican family rhetoric moves unmistakably to the right. After making relatively liberal pledges about using government to help disadvantaged families in the 1950s and 1960s, the Republican Party began to argue that the government is antithetical to the interests of parents and threatens the very existence of the family. Essentially, the Republicans increasingly co-opt the language of family to frame and strengthen their agenda of smaller government, lower taxes, and fewer regulations (see table 3.4).

Not surprisingly, the earliest policy singled out for critique by the Republicans was Aid to Families with Dependent Children (welfare), which in 1992 the party declared to be "anti-work and anti-marriage. It taxes families to subsidize illegitimacy." In his 1992 State of the Union address, President George H. W. Bush explicitly framed opposition to welfare as pro-parent. He said, "Ask American parents what they dislike about how things are going in our country, and chances are good that pretty soon they'll get to welfare." Beyond welfare, a broad range of government programs, regulations, and actions were framed as threatening the survival of the family. A White House working group on the family created by President Reagan concluded that "big government is harmful to families" (Wisensale 1997, 79). Republicans also began

Table 3.4. Partisan Uses of Family and Parent Language to Frame Governing Philosophy

Republican Party	Democratic Party

Government may be strong enough to destroy families, but it can never replace them.
   —1980 Republican platform
	Our next great goal should be to strengthen our families. I compliment the Congress for passing the Family and Medical Leave Act as a good first step, but it is time to do more.
	   —Clinton 1993 State of the Union

For more than three decades, the liberal philosophy has assaulted the family on every side.
   —1992 Republican platform
 	
The liberal democrats want power in the hands of the federal government. I want power in the hands of parents.
   —Bush 1988 convention speech
	To me, family values means. . . . Putting both Social Security and Medicare in an iron-clad lock box. . . . Getting cigarettes out of the hands of kids before they get hooked. . . . A new prescription drug benefit under Medicare for all our seniors. . . . We will honor families by expanding child care, and after-school care, and family and medical leave—so working parents have the help they need to care for their children.
	   —Gore 2000 convention speech

We pledge comprehensive tax reform that will give America back what was its post-war glory: a pro-family tax code.
   —1984 Republican platform
 	
We seek to minimize the financial burdens imposed by government upon families.
   —1988 Republican platform
	You don't value families by kicking kids out of after school programs. . . . You don't value families by denying real prescription drug coverage to seniors. . . . We believe in the family value expressed in one of the oldest Commandments: "Honor thy father and thy mother." As President, I will not privatize Social Security.
	   —Kerry 2004 convention speech

Regulatory costs are now running in excess of $100 billion each year, or about $1,800 for every American family.

—1980 Republican platform

But when we deregulate, let's remember what national action in the national interest has given us: safer foods for our families, safer toys for our children, safer nursing homes for our parents, safer cars and highways, and safer workplaces, clean air and cleaner water.

— Clinton, 1995 State of the Union

American families with children are the hardest hit during any economic downturn. Republicans will lower their tax burden.

—2008 Republican platform

We Democrats want—and we hereby pledge—a government led by Barack Obama that looks out for families in the new economy with health care, retirement security, and help, especially in bad times.

—2008 Democratic platform

to condemn big government for infringing on the sacred ground of parental authority, while charging that the Democratic Party sought to usurp the role of parents and the family through the expansion of government actions and programs. In their 2008 platform, the Republicans make a simple reaffirmation that "As the family is our basic unit in society, we oppose initiatives to erode parental rights."

The Republicans also began to argue that tax cuts were the best way to honor and strengthen families. In the 1950s and 1960s such rhetoric was not entirely absent from Republican rhetoric, but was quite different in its prominence. For example, the 1956 Republican platform states "the American wage earner today can buy more than ever before for himself and his family because his pay check has not been eaten away by rising taxes and soaring prices." This statement is typical of this time period in its almost offhand reference to the family. In contrast, starting in the 1980s the party began to emphatically frame tax cut proposals of all kinds as "pro-family" and concrete steps to strengthen the American family. This theme is emphasized even more heavily in 2008 in response to tougher economic times. The 2008 Republican platform states that "American families with children are the hardest hit during any economic downturn" and that "Republicans will lower their tax burden." In a section of the platform titled "The Democrats Plan to Raise Your Taxes" the party explains that the impact of rolling back the Bush tax cuts would be "disastrous" for families.

Republicans not only come to herald conservative economic positions as quintessential pro-family policy, they framed their new and expanding conservative social agenda in family-friendly terms. After decades of using "family" in a rather offhand way, the Republican Party makes it clear it is interested in protecting one particular type of family, the traditional family composed of "a mother and father anchored by the bonds of marriage." Starting in 1980 and continuing through the present, Republicans highlight their commitment to traditional family values and appointing judges who uphold such values. The 1992 Republican Convention designated an entire evening as "Family Values Night," values which they defined as conservative, religious ones.[4] The 1992 platform announced that "Republicans oppose and resist the efforts of the Democratic Party to redefine the traditional American family" and, for the first time, articulated the party's opposition to same-sex marriage and adoption, while supporting the right of the Boy Scouts to exclude gays. In his 2004 State of the Union address President George W. Bush endorsed a constitutional amendment to ban gay marriage arguing that such an action was critical to keeping America's families and the nation strong. In a similar vein, the 2008 Republican platform states that "Given the weight of social science evidence concerning the crucial role played by the traditional family in setting a child's future course, we urge a thoughtful review of government policies and programs to ensure that they do not undermine the institution."

The Republican Party also started articulating more conservative rhetoric and policies concerning women and mothers. As Christina Wolbrecht argues in her detailed analysis of partisan realignment over women's issues, the Republican Party began "distancing itself from feminists and siding with those who prefer more traditional women's roles" (2000, 3). Starting in 1980, Republicans dropped their support for the Equal Rights Amendment and in its place began championing the vital and underappreciated role of mothers and homemakers in maintaining the health of the nation. While the party does not vilify working mothers (Sanbonmatsu 2004), it also not so subtly emphasizes the desirability of more traditional roles for women. The 1992 platform accuses Democrats of "forcing millions of women into the workplace" and declares that "the well-being of children is best accomplished in the environment of the home" not in child care centers. The party also has opposed policies, including the Family and Medical Leave Act and publicly funded child care, aimed to support working mothers.

The flip side of Republican rhetoric valuing traditional families is rhetoric devaluing single parents. The party has made it clear that "The two-parent family still provides the best environment of stability, discipline, responsibility, and character" and that people have a "responsibility to hold their families together and refrain from having children out of wedlock."[5] In his 1996 presidential nomination acceptance speech, Bob Dole labeled "illegitimacy" and "abandonment of children" as two of the major problems plaguing America along with crime, drugs, abortion, and abandonment of duty. In stark contrast to rhetoric recognizing the value of homemakers, Republicans demand that those on welfare, disproportionately single mothers, enter the workforce and work more hours. Starting under Reagan, calls for tougher enforcement of parental support payments become a regular theme in Republican appeals.

The Republican Party also began championing a new set of social regulatory policies to protect the family from what it perceived to be harmful influences. The party started adding sections to its platforms titled "Family Protection" under which it articulates its unequivocal opposition to abortion and support for a range of government actions and policies to outlaw the practice. Similarly, the party began endorsing legislation to regulate the media and access to the internet arguing such policies support parental authority and protect children. In his 1984 State of the Union address, Reagan said, "Parents need to know their children will not be victims of child pornography and abduction." In the

2000 platform the party endorses legislation "to require schools and libraries to secure their computers against on-line porn and predators."

Finally, although much less prominent than in their discussions of social policy, the Republicans also lean on parent-family themes to communicate their national security and war policy to the nation. Although references to military families appear in speeches and platforms in prior decades, they become more common in the twenty-first century. President George W. Bush references parents, family, and children to highlight achievements in Afghanistan and to rally support for and then defend the invasion of Iraq. In 2002 Bush stated, "This [Iraq] is a regime that has already used poison gas to murder thousands of its own citizens—leaving the bodies of mothers huddled over their dead children." In 2003 he says, "Iraqi refugees tell us how forced confessions are obtained: by torturing children while their parents are made to watch." Although the war on terrorism does not become the dominant use of such references, it comes close in 2002, when eleven out of eighteen of Bush's parent-family references in his State of the Union address were connected to such themes. Ferguson (2004) has analyzed the way President Bush used women's rights language and concerns to promote the war on terrorism in both Afghanistan and Iraq. Our analysis shows that parents and the family have become frames for such policies as well.

In summary, over the past three decades, parenthood and the family have emerged as a central theme in Republican discourse. References to parents and family changed from being colloquial ways of referring to struggling farmers or poor people in American society, to both *forming and framing* the heart of the party's domestic agenda. What was new was not the Republican Party's belief in smaller government and tax cuts, but the aggressive way the party came to use parent and family frames to market these core beliefs. In addition, the Republican Party came to embrace a whole new set of social regulatory policies designed to protect and preserve the traditional family. Rather than appealing to society to help disadvantaged families, the Republicans began to appeal directly to middle-class, married parents, pitching everything from tax cuts to anti-abortion legislation as a way to strengthen parental rights and autonomy and to help parents protect their children from illicit societal influences.

Democrats: Government Action Needed to Help Working Parents and Families

The Democrats, just like the Republicans, began to devote prominent space in their platforms and national addresses to emphasizing the health of the family as a fundamental basis for their policy prescriptions, but moved in this direction about twelve years after the Republicans. Jimmy Carter was, in fact, the first president to mention the need to strengthen the family in his inaugural address, but this did not become a central theme in Democratic communication until 1992. As president, Bill Clinton not only continued to praise the family in the same manner as his Republican predecessors, but brought such rhetoric to new heights. The need to protect and strengthen the family was a central theme in every one of Clinton's State of the Union addresses, as well as his two convention speeches. Typical is this statement from his 1996 State of the Union address: "Our first challenge is to cherish our children and strengthen America's families. Family is the foundation of American life. If we have stronger families, we will have a stronger America." Although it is clear that Clinton was a major force behind this shift in rhetoric, this emphasis became a regular part of Democratic Party communications and continued through the convention speeches of Al Gore, John Kerry, and Barack Obama. The 2004 Democratic platform, for example, stated that "strong families—blessed with opportunity, committed to responsibility, and filled with dreams—are the heart of a stronger America."

While the Democratic emphasis on strengthening families echoes that of Republicans, the policy proposals Democrats offered to achieve this end were, more often than not, the party's reliance on government-based social welfare programs. The Democratic Party explicitly co-opted the language of family to push for expanded social welfare programs, more government regulations of business and the economy, and a larger role for the government overall—positions diametrically opposed to the pro-family policies advocated by Republicans. The polarization can be clearly seen on policies closely connected to parenthood and children such as the Family and Medical Leave Act, which allows parents to take unpaid leave after the birth or adoption of a child. After President George H. W. Bush vetoed this legislation twice, Bill Clinton not only signed it into law as one of his first acts as president, but spent the rest of his presidency championing its passage and the need for its expansion, arguing that it was an essential pro-family and pro-parent policy—a theme continued by his successors. Additionally, the party continued to push for increased spending on child care, after school and summer school programs, and Head Start, arguing, as Al Gore did in 2000, that such policies "honor families" and epitomize real family values. Especially after the failure of Clinton's universal health care proposal, Democrats actively framed new government health care proposals, such as the Children's Health Initiative Program (CHIP), which covered children of the working poor, as well as a plan to cover the unemployed, as pro-family.

The language of children and families is also used to advocate for a robust role of government in areas beyond those directly affecting parents and children, such as an increase in the minimum wage. In 2000 Al Gore explicitly defines "family values" as protecting social security and Medicare and passing a new drug benefit for seniors. Likewise, John Kerry in 2004 argues that the maintenance and expansion of government social welfare programs are the true way to "value families." In their 2008 platform, Democrats argued that the best way to help America's working parents through economically challenging times was through increased government action to provide universal health care, ensure Americans get good jobs with good pay, preserve social security, and combat poverty. Similar to Republicans, what is new is not the positions the party took about the need for an active government, but the way the party came to market these positions as pro-parent and pro-family.

Democrats also increasingly made the case that government regulations of the economy and of business are pro-family and support family values. In 1995, Clinton stated, "let's remember what national action in the national interest has given us: safer foods for our families, safer toys for our children, safer nursing homes for our parents, safer cars and highways, and safer workplaces, clean airs and cleaner water." In 2000 Gore announced that "Getting cigarettes out of the hands of kids before they get hooked is a family value. I will crack down on the marketing of tobacco to our children." He went on to define family values as not only fighting against big tobacco, but also fighting big oil, big polluters, pharmaceutical companies, and HMOs. Starting in the 1990s, environmental regulations are also pitched as pro-parent. In the 2004 platform support for a range of environmental regulations and policies is placed under the section titled "The Family." Finally, as others have pointed out, the Democratic Party came to frame their support of women's rights issues, including tougher enforcement of equal pay laws, in terms of family and mothers (Freeman 1997; Sanbonmatsu 2004). In a noteworthy contrast to Republicans who clearly situated their pro-life position on abortion as one of their pro-family policies, Democrats make a concerted effort to separate their pro-choice position on abortion from their family rhetoric.

In the Democratic Party's most recent communications with the public, family frames to promote government action are most prominent when discussing the economic crisis. In his 2009 address to the joint session of Congress, President Obama emphasized that swift and aggressive government action was needed so "families can afford to buy homes" and to "help responsible families facing the threat of foreclosure." In the 2008 platform, the Democrats emphasize that while government is always needed to help America's working families, this responsibility is heightened in a rough economy. "We Democrats want—and we hereby pledge—a government led by Barack Obama that looks out for families in the new economy with health care, retirement security, and help, especially in bad times."

The language of the Democratic Party shifts in one additional and very important way when relating to the government's role. The Democratic Party comes to replace pledges to help low-income families and poor parents, which were pervasive in the public statements of Democrats in prior decades, with pledges to help working parents and middle-class families. The change was not purely rhetorical either, as it was accompanied by Clinton signing welfare reform into law in 1996. In his convention speech that year Clinton held up welfare reform as representing a "new social bargain with the poor," where poor children would be helped through social welfare programs but not their parents. Thus, the Democrats appear to make a strategic choice in the 1990s, to *not* be the party of poor parents and families. Rather, working parents, working families, and middle-class families become the new marginalized group that needs government intervention and for which the Democrats must fight—groups, of course, that have much broader political appeal and power.

While the core of the Democrats' pro-family policies is diametrically opposed to those of Republicans, starting in the 1990s, the Democratic Party moves rightward to embrace several social policy positions similar to those of the Republican Party. Clinton not only followed Reagan's lead in rebuking parents for delinquent child support payments, but made such themes a centerpiece of his presidential agenda. At the 1992 Democratic convention Clinton said, "I do want to say something to the fathers in this country who have chosen to abandon their children by neglecting their child support: Take responsibility for your children or we will force you to do so. Because governments don't raise children; parents do." During his second term, Clinton called for even tougher legislation making it a felony for deadbeat parents to cross state lines. Barack Obama emphasized these themes heavily in his 2008 presidential campaign and his first term as president. In addition to devoting an entire national address to the issue of fatherhood and responsibility on Father's Day in 2008, his 2008 convention speech stated "that fathers must take more responsibility for providing the love and guidance their children need" and that "[government] programs alone can't replace parents." For the first time, the 2008 Democratic platform devoted an entire section to "Fatherhood," which not only implored fathers to become more responsible and involved, but also laid out a series of government programs to support fathers in these efforts including "providing transition training to get jobs" and "expanding maternity and paternity leave."

Under Clinton, the Democratic Party also unfurled a range of proposals to increase parental authority and help parents protect their children from negative cultural influences. Clinton admonished the entertainment industry to create movies, music, and television with child-appropriate content, and to rate televisions shows "in ways that help parents protect their children." He championed the V-chip, which enabled "parents to assume more personal responsibility for their children's upbringing."[6] Similar to the Republicans, the Democrats pitched such social regulations directly to parents. For example, in 2000, Al Gore spoke directly "To all the families who are struggling with things that money can't measure—like trying to find a little more time to spend with your children" and pledged to "stand with you for a goal that we share: to give more power back to the parents, to choose what your own children are exposed to, so you can pass on your family's basic lessons of responsibility and decency." In his 2009 address to the joint session of Congress, President Obama stated that "In the end, there is no program or policy that can substitute for a mother or father who will attend those parent/teacher conferences, or help with homework after dinner, or turn off the TV, put away the video games, and read to their child. I speak to you not just as a President, but as a father when I say that responsibility for our children's education must begin at home."

Democrats also reposition their rhetoric about family structure, so that it is more moderate than liberal. In the 1980s, the Democratic Party cited the need to make "federal programs more sensitive to the needs of the family, in all its diverse forms" and critically stated that "In Ronald Reagan's vision of America, there are no single parent families, women only stay at home and care for children."[7] Starting in 1992, however, Democrats pair such inclusive rhetoric with more conservative language. Democrats concede that one-mother-one-father-married parents are superior, although the Democratic language is not as strident as that used by the Republican Party. In his 1996 State of the Union address Clinton stated, "I challenge America's families to work harder to stay together. For families who stay together not only do better economically, their children do better as well." Democrats also seek out decidedly middle ground on gay rights and feminist issues, stopping short of supporting full rights for same-sex families and replacing feminist frames with more palatable family frames in its discussion of women's rights issues.

The extension of parent-family language to the war in Iraq in the years following the 9-11 terrorist attacks has been a bipartisan phenomenon as well. In his 2004 convention speech, John Kerry used parent-family language to criticize Bush's Iraq policy and frame his own plan. He stated that "You don't value families if you force them to take up a collection to buy body armor for a son or daughter in the service" and also said, "As President, I will wage this war with the lessons I learned in war. Before you go to battle, you have to be able to look a parent in the eye and truthfully say: 'I tried everything possible to avoid sending your son or daughter into harm's way.' " The 2004 Democratic platform devotes a section to "Standing Up for Military Families" and speaks of the parties desire to enact a "Military Family Bill of Rights."

Strategic Parties and the Use of Parent-Family Themes

Public discussions about parenthood and family are not new. Historical studies show that "protection of the family has been a powerful motif among reformers since the origins of mass politics before the Civil War" (Ribuffo 2006, 311–312). Similarly, in her book *Embattled Paradise*, sociologist Arlene Skolnick points out that "The rhetoric of family crises has persisted as a theme in our culture for more than a century" (1991, xix). What is new, according to the quantitative analyses presented in this chapter, is the degree to which the language of parenthood and the family drives political discourse.

In their totality, our analyses of speeches and platforms show that parenthood and the family have become significantly politicized. Over the last half century, parenthood and the family have gone from being essentially non-political and non-partisan issues—rarely being mentioned in platforms, speeches, presidential campaigns—to providing a central frame for the broad domestic policy agendas of both parties as well as being the center of a new policy focus. Although there has been a slight decline in parent-family references thus far in the twenty-first century, they remain dominant themes in the communications of the parties and their standard-bearers with the public. Given that only a tiny fraction of all possible issues make it onto the political agenda, it is all the more significant that parenthood and the family have become unusually persistent "leading themes" of American electoral politics (Carmines and Stimson 1989, 3). The parties and their leaders have clearly come to believe that the "family frame" is an effective way to compete for public opinion and voters across a wide variety of issues.

Although the politicization of parenthood and the family has been bipartisan, the essential core of the parties' pro-family policies has polarized, reflecting the widening cleavage between the parties over the proper role of government. Despite Barack Obama's claims of being post-partisan, he uses the language of the family in very much the same ways as his immediate predecessors on the Democratic side in which he skillfully recasts policies at the heart of the Democratic message since the New Deal as pro-family policies. On the Republican side, both the party's platform and its 2008 standard-bearer, John McCain, relied heavily on parent-family language to justify traditional Republican positions on economic policy, emphasizing that tax increases and bigger government during the economic downturn would be disastrous for American families. Although they are diametrically opposing positions, Jacoby (2000) has shown that framed correctly both of these messages about the appropriate role of government are supported by a majority of the public.

In the realm of social and cultural issues the parties' pro-family messages are less polarized and this makes strategic sense as well. Republicans were pushed to embrace conservative family rhetoric and policies by one particular "unsatisfied constituency," social conservatives deeply concerned about the dramatic changes characterizing the American family. Rather than polarizing on this set of issues, the Democrats triangulated by embracing parental authority, rebuking deadbeat dads, castigating the media to provide more child-appropriate content, dropping their explicit support of poor single parents, and refusing to embrace gay marriage. These positions make strategic sense as well considering that the majority of Americans have concerns about the decline of the traditional family and remain ambivalent or opposed to more progressive or alternative family arrangements (Sanbonmatsu 2004; Pew Research Center 2010). While the particular contours of the partisan evolution around issues of the family make strategic sense, the parties' decision to highlight and in many respects glorify not only families, but a particular type of families—middle-class families headed by married parents—holds some troubling consequences for the representation of poorer families, single parents, and women, which we explore in our concluding chapter.

The findings presented in this chapter are significant not only because they reveal an interesting evolution within the American party system, but because they have the potential to shape the broader political and electoral context in multiple ways. First, the increasing use of parent and family themes by the political parties and their presidential candidates holds the potential to drive the news media to embrace such frames as well. While media coverage of presidential campaigns does not follow the "campaign model of reporting" where the media take their cues directly from candidates (Patterson 1993, chapter 4), studies have shown that the messages coming from the parties and their presidential campaigns do heavily influence the content of news coverage (Jamieson 2000, chapter 25). Trends in the ways the new media have embraced themes of parenthood and the family in their electoral coverage is the subject of the next chapter.

Additionally, the politicization of parenthood and the family shape the political context by setting the stage for the politicization of actual parents. Research has shown that the issues the parties and political leaders choose to emphasize and how they talk about those issues has significant impact on public opinion and political behavior. In his analysis of State of the Union addresses from 1953 to 1989, Cohen (1995) found that the more presidents mention certain problems or policy areas, irrespective of the substance of those references, the more concerned the public becomes with those topics (Cohen 1995, 102).[8] Similarly, Sanbonmatsu argues that "By calling attention to certain issues in their campaigns, candidates seek to make voters choose on the basis of that issue" (2004, 115). The implication is that the more the parties, presidents, and presidential nominees talk about parents and families, the more likely people are to invoke their parenthood identification when thinking about political issues. The ways in which parents are or are not distinctive in their political attitudes is the focus of chapters 5 and 6.

4

The Rise of Politicized Moms and Dads

Media Coverage of Parenthood

The last chapter revealed that parenthood and the family have gone from being essentially non-political and non-partisan issues—rarely being mentioned in platforms, major speeches, and presidential campaigns—to providing a fundamental frame for the broad domestic policy agendas of both parties and providing the basis for new policy initiatives explicitly directed toward parents. In this chapter, we turn to the news media, a central actor in contemporary elections and the main source of political information for the American public. To make our analysis of the news media as parallel as possible to our analysis of elite political communications documented in the previous chapter, we analyze news coverage of elections from 1952 through the present, systematically documenting the media's use of parent-family labels in their election coverage. We also explore the policy focus of all the news articles using parent-family frames. The results build a rich picture of not only *how much*, but also *how* the news media have talked about parents and families in their political coverage. While a few studies have examined the use of one particular parent-family theme in one particular election year, such as "family values" in 1992 or "Soccer Moms" in 1996, this chapter provides the first systematic exploration of the media's use of all parent-family language over the last half century.

The Politicization of Parenthood and the
Family in the Media

The first goal of the media analysis was to explore whether the news media have "politicized" parenthood and the family over the last half century. In other words, have the news media increasingly used parents and families as frames in their election coverage? To answer this question we conducted a content analysis of two print news sources from 1952 through the 2008 election. The primary source for our media analysis is the *New York Times*, although we conduct a parallel analysis using *Time* magazine. We chose to use these two news sources because they are widely read, influential sources of information (Jamieson and Waldman 2003, 96–97), and on a practical level, they have been in existence in a fairly consistent format across the long time period of our study and have searchable archives going back through 1952. Additionally, the *New York Times* and *Time* have been used by other scholars in their content analyses of political and election news coverage (Carroll 1999, 2008; Gilens 1999; Patterson 1993; Wattenberg 1998). Although it is hard to make the case that any one or two sources are representative of all news media, scholars have pointed out that there are more similarities than differences in presidential election coverage across media platforms and sources (Graber 2006, 232; Kerbel, Apee, and Ross 2000).

Following Susan Carroll's approach (1999, 2008) in her content analysis of the media's use of the terms "Soccer Moms" during the 1996 election and "Security Moms" in the 2004 election, we searched news archives across the time period of July 1 through November 30 in each presidential election year from 1952 through 2008. This time frame captures news coverage of both major party conventions as well as wrap-up coverage after the election, but avoids primary coverage, which might be weighted more heavily toward one party or the other depending on which side had a more competitive or drawn-out contest. Using the Proquest Historical archive of the *New York Times* and Lexis/Nexis, we identified all articles that had the keywords "presidential election(s)" along with one or more of the following: "parent(s)," "mother(s)/mom(s)," "father(s)/dad(s)," "family/families," and "children/kid(s)" in the article headline or lead paragraph. We conducted a parallel search and analysis using *Time* magazine. Articles in which references to parent-family terms were made offhandedly or in a non-political context were discarded. For example, articles referring to the candidates' parents were not coded for this study. Articles were included in our analysis only if parents, families, and/or children formed a major focus or frame in the article's discussion of politics, elections, and/or policy. Letters to the editor as well as transcripts of debates or speeches were eliminated, but editorials were kept as these are some of the most widely read and discussed elements within news publications. We refer to the articles that met all our criteria as having parent-family themes and report the results of our analysis in table 4.2. As a result of *Time* being a weekly rather than daily news source, the year-by-year figures are generally too small for meaningful analysis, so we rely solely on the *New York Times* data as the basis for figures and tables besides table 4.2

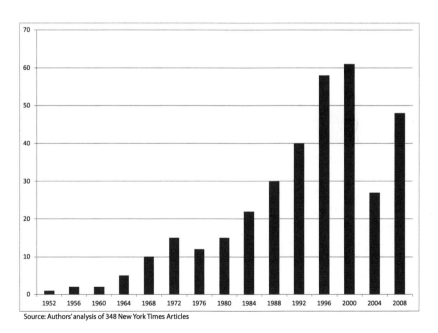

Source: Authors' analysis of 348 New York Times Articles

Figure 4.1. News Stories with Parent-Family Themes by Presidential Election Year.

The results show that the news media have indeed politicized parenthood and the family. Figure 4.1 shows the number of news stories with parent-family themes from 1952 through the 2008 election and illustrates an overall upward trend, despite a sizable decrease in 2004. Despite the dominance of traditional families in the American social landscape throughout the 1950s and 1960s, the results in figure 4.1 quite clearly show that the topics of parent-hood and the family were not themes in political coverage during those decades. There was only one *New York Times* article in 1952 and two articles in 1956 that adopted parent-family frames. The figures for the 1960s are slightly, but not much, higher. Since then, parent-family themes have become strikingly more common in election coverage. The number of articles employing parent-family frames close to doubles across each of the following decades throughout the twentieth century, peaking at sixty-one in 2000. Media coverage of the 2004 election, the first presidential election after the September 11, 2001 terrorist attacks, was heavily focused on national security issues, a policy area in which parent-family frames are less common. As a result, the number of articles using parent-family frames dropped down to twenty-seven, a twenty-year low. The 2008 presidential election, however, shows a strong rebound in the media's use of parent-family themes, the third highest in our fifty-six-year analysis. Table 4.1 displays the results of regression analysis indicating that the upward trend in the use of parent-family themes is not only substantively significant, but statistically significant over time.

Table 4.1. OLS Regression of Number of Articles by Year, 1952–2008

Year	.996***
	(.15)
Number	15
Adjusted R^2	.76

Cell entry is regression coefficient and the Standard Error is in parentheses.
***$p<.001$

The first three columns in table 4.2 shows the breakdown of the *Time* articles by election year compared to the *New York Times* and reveals significant upward trends in both news sources. *Time* had no parent-family-themed election stories throughout the 1950s and peaked at eleven in 1996, the year that "Soccer Moms," V-chips, and parental responsibility were prominent themes in partisan discourse. In *Time* coverage, the 2008 election tied with 1992 as having the second highest number of election articles employing parent-family themes. The upward trends documented in table 4.2 reinforce results from similar media analyses employing less stringent standards for article inclusion (Elder and Greene 2006).[1]

A striking characteristic about the politicization of parenthood and the family by the news media is the degree to which the increases mirror the trend in the communications of political

Table 4.2. Articles with Parent-Family Themes by Year

Year	NYT Total	Time Total	*Family*	*Parent*	*Mother/ mom*	*Father/ dad*	*Child/ kids*
1952	1	0	0	0	1	0	1
1956	2	0	1	0	0	1	2
1960	2	1	1	0	1	2	1
1964	5	1	4	1	0	0	2
1968	10	2	7	4	2	1	8
1972	15	2	13	3	1	0	9
1976	12	3	8	1	3	0	7
1980	15	2	10	4	6	1	9
1984	22	5	19	4	3	1	7
1988	30	3	25	13	5	1	21
1992	40	7	36	10	12	1	27
1996	58	11	47	25	17	3	45
2000	61	3	42	21	4	1	42
2004	27	5	22	4	5	2	14
2008	48	7	36	17	20	6	31

Cell entries are number of articles overall and numbers of *NYT* articles using particular parent-family terms.

Source: *New York Times* and *Time* magazine.

parties and elites revealed in the prior chapter. Figure 4.2 combines results from the previous chapter with the news media analysis, so as to illustrate the strongly parallel trends. In the 1950s and 1960s neither the political parties, nor the news media, were discussing parents, families, or children in their communications to the public. Between 1972 and 1988 the number of *New York Times* stories with parent-family themes doubled, as does the usage of parent-family language in the platforms of both political parties. News stories with family and parent themes peak in the last decade of the twentieth century, the same decade that references to parent-family terms peak in platforms as well as convention and State of the Union addresses. The absolute high in news articles with parent-family themes was in 2000, the same year parent-family references in party platforms hit their all-time high. This is also the same year parent-family references in convention speeches peaked, when Al Gore and George W. Bush collectively made 152 family-parent references when accepting their parties' presidential nominations. Finally, in both elite rhetoric and the print news media there is a decline in parent-family themes in 2004 reflecting the shifting focus from the domestic arena to the international arena and a rebound in the 2008 election, although the news media coverage rebounded more quickly and strongly than rhetoric from parties and candidates.

Figure 4.3 and the last columns in table 4.2 break down the results by specific parent-family terms and show that despite the drop in 2004 the general upward trend holds true for each term analyzed. Despite all the attention catchy labels have drawn to motherhood, with terms such as "Soccer Moms" and "Security Moms," the results show that it is not just motherhood that has become politicized, but families, parents, and children as well. In fact, of all the parent-family terms examined, the most common was "family/families" followed by "children/kids," "parents," and "mothers."

Although fathers are still mentioned the least of all the parent-family terms, 2008 election coverage represents the fifty-six-year high in the media's usage of this term. The significant uptick in election articles using "father frames" was driven in part by media coverage of Barack Obama's emphasis on the need for fathers to become more involved in their children's lives, as discussed in the previous chapter. The 2008 presidential election also represented

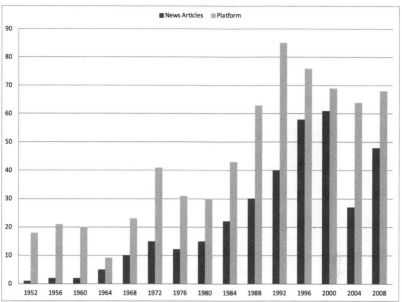

Source: Authors' analysis of 348 New York Times Articles. Platform figure represents the number of references to parent-family terms adjusted for length of platform.

Figure 4.2. Party and Media Use of Parent-Family Themes.

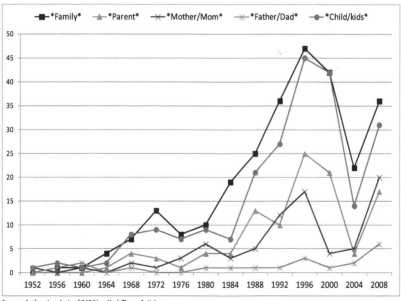

Source: Authors' analysis of 348 New York Times Articles

Figure 4.3. Articles with Parent-Family Themes and Terminology.

a fifty-six-year highpoint in election articles using "mothers" as news frames. Many of these articles discussed the electoral implications of Sarah Palin's status as a mother of five children and her frequent self-references in her speeches to being a "Hockey Mom." Although the news media have used parent-based labels such as "Soccer Moms" for many electoral cycles, this is the first time one of the party's standard-bearers used these terms herself, thus explicitly driving the media's usage of the term. Other "mom" labels that appeared in 2008 election coverage were "Walmart Moms" and "Mortgage Moms." In other words, the media relied on mother-based labels as ways to increase the attractiveness of their reporting on the economic, tax, and regulatory proposals of the candidates, the issues that were most important to voters in the 2008 election. The fact that mothers remained the subject of so many more election stories than fathers is revealing of the continued gendered expectations and realities of parenting, as discussed in chapter 2. Moreover, the heavier reliance on motherhood frames and labels also reflects the fact that motherhood remains a more powerful and controversial symbol in American society (Douglas and Michaels 2004), making it a more attractive frame for news stories.

Media Coverage of Parenthood and Policy Issues

In addition to analyzing the number of parent and family themed stories, we also wanted to understand the content of these stories and more specifically to explore what issues the news media use parent-family language to frame. Given the parties' integration of parent-family themes into an ever-widening array of policy issues, we were interested in understanding what issues the news media used parent-family frames to discuss and whether the issues changed over time. First, we determined whether each article had a substantive policy focus or not. Interestingly, despite criticism of the overload of "horse-race coverage" and a dearth of substantive issue discussions in election coverage (Patterson 2000, 1993), the vast majority of parent-family election articles addressed one or more policy issues. Each news article was then individually coded as to what policy issue(s) was/were most prominently discussed in the article using the following categories: policies to help poor families/parents; economic policy/tax cuts; government programs for children; government social welfare programs not explicitly for children; economic regulation; cultural values policies; protecting children; war/national security/foreign policy; other (see appendix 1 for a more detailed description of these categories). Articles that mentioned more than one policy area were coded positively for each policy area.

Figure 4.4 presents the number of parent-family-themed articles focusing on each policy area across time. Taken as a whole, this figure illustrates that journalists are not just employing parent-family themes to discuss issues directly related to children, but as a way of assessing the central policy proposals and differences of the major parties. Besides issues dealing directly with children (e.g., education, child care, health care programs for children), the top issue foci of these articles are the economy, social welfare issues,

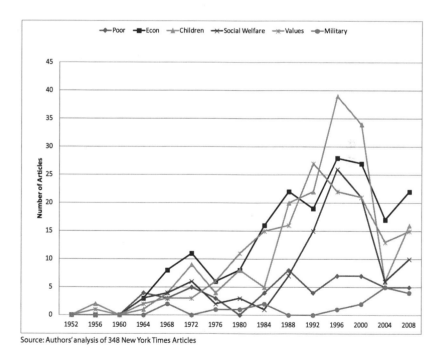

Source: Authors' analysis of 348 New York Times Articles

Figure 4.4. Central Issue Focus of Parent-Family Themed Articles Over Time.

and values issues. These issues not only form the heart of the partisan divisions in American politics, but represent the most salient issues during recent elections.

To a large degree, the policy focus of the news articles parallels the substance of partisan rhetoric discussed in the previous chapter where we found that when the words "family" and "parenthood" were evoked in elite rhetoric in the 1950s and 1960s, these terms were used to frame a narrow set of issues: the concerns of low-income families and programs geared to help disadvantaged children. While it is hard to identify any issue themes coming from the 1950s and 1960s since the population of articles is so small, most election stories concerning parents, families, and children focused on these policy areas. The election of 1964, for example, is the only election year where poverty is the top policy focus of parent-family election articles. Articles with a poverty focus represent a declining share of parent-family-themed election articles over time reflecting, in part, the changing rhetoric of politicians, who have shifted their focus more toward "middle-class" and "working" families.

Across the last half century, the most common issue focus of the parent-family-themed news article has been the economy. In fact, the number of articles focusing on the economy surpasses the number focused on children's issues in all decades except the 1990s and represents the top policy theme in election years when the economy was the most important issue. The economy was discussed in 69 percent of parent-family-themed articles in the 1980s. This is the decade when the Republican Party, under the leadership of Ronald Reagan, began aggressively promoting tax cuts and less government spending as pro-family policies. In 2008, there was a substantive rise in stories with parent-family themes that focus on the economy, which is not surprising given the economic climate during the election. In 2008, 46 percent (twenty-two of the forty-eight) election articles using parent-family frames focused on the economy, which was more than any other issue area.

The second most frequent policy area addressed in parent-family themed articles is, not surprisingly, policies dealing with government spending and programs designed to help parents care for their children including: child care, education, the Family and Medical Leave Act, and college tuition/loans. Not that far behind in terms of numbers are articles about government social welfare programs not directly related to children including Social Security, health care, Medicare, and Medicaid. Here too the media appears to have followed the lead of political elites. As the Democratic Party began to co-opt the language of parenthood and family values to push for expanded social welfare programs, and the Republican Party increasingly argued that government programs take power away from parents and undermine families, the number of news articles embracing parent-family themes to discuss social welfare programs increased.

The third most frequently mentioned issue area is values, which includes articles discussing family values, traditional families, the appropriate role for mothers, abortion, gay marriage, and stem cells. While values-related discussions were not absent from parent-family-themed articles in the 1950s, 1960s, and 1970s, their numbers jump upward in the 1980s and remain quite high throughout the 1990s. Once again this is in keeping with the partisan rhetoric described in the previous chapter. Not surprisingly the one election year where values outnumber all other issues is the 1992 election, the first year the Republican Party explicitly articulated opposition to same-sex marriage and same-sex adoption in its platform, and designated an entire night at its convention as "Family Values Night." The 1990s are also the decade that Democrats, especially President Bill Clinton, start admonishing families to stay together, fathers to become more responsible, and the media to do a better job of protecting kids.

As figure 4.4 shows, parent-family frames have rarely been used to discuss military or national security issues. Although the number of election articles with parent-family themes declined significantly in the wake of the September 11, 2001 terrorist attacks, it is not surprising to find that a greater number of parent-family-themed articles discussed national security / defense in 2004 than in any other election year. This increase reflects the prominence of the media's new parent label, "Security Moms," as well as efforts by the parties to frame their national security agendas as providing more protection for families. Throughout the 1990s only 1 percent of parent-family articles dealt with defense or military issues, but in 2004 close to one in five did. At the same time, it is important to note though that "Security Moms" and defense issue stories remained significantly fewer than those discussing families in the context of the economy and values, even in 2004.

The previous chapter showed that despite conventional wisdom that the Republican Party has been the driver of the debate over family values, the Democratic Party kept up with their Republican counterparts and in quite a few years even surpassed them in their use of parent-family themes. Given this, we were interested in seeing whether the media were more likely to associate the themes of parenthood and the family with one of the major political parties more than the other. To measure the partisan leanings of the media references we coded each parent-family-themed article as to whether it mentioned either or both of the Democratic or Republican parties and/or candidates.

Table 4.3 shows the results of this analysis. As a group, the 348 parent-family-themed election articles from the *New York Times* are highly partisan. An overwhelming 97 percent of the articles mention one or both parties. While some have warned about the declining prominence of political parties in election coverage (Wattenberg 1998), these results document a strong, consistent presence of both parties in election-related stories with parent-family themes. Table 4.3 also shows that the two major parties show up roughly equally in news articles. Three-fourths of the articles mention both parties, and among the seventy-one stories

Table 4.3. Political Party Mentioned in Parent-Family-Themed Articles

	Number of articles
Stories mentioning neither party	11
Stories mentioning both parties	266
Stories mentioning Republicans only	33
Stories mentioning Democrats only	38

Source: Authors' analysis of 348 *New York Times* articles.

that only mentioned one party, 42 percent mentioned Republicans and 58 percent mentioned Democrats.

Figure 4.5 displays the partisan breakdown of the articles by election year from 1952 through 2008. Throughout the 1980s, and then again in 2004 and 2008, Republicans show up in articles slightly more often than Democrats, and the reverse is true in 1996 and 2000. The central story of figure 4.5, however, is one of party parity rather than one of party disparity. The roughly equal coverage given to both parties in parent-family-themed news articles reflects the roughly equal attention the parties themselves have given to parent-family themes. This means that neither party has a "leg up" on the other in terms of being associated with parents and families in election coverage.

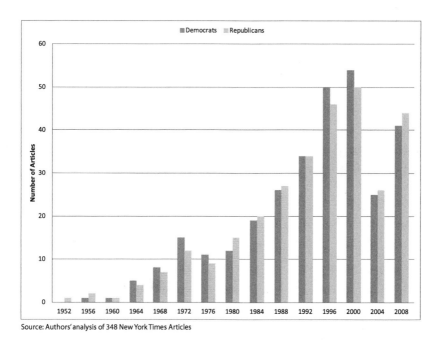

Source: Authors' analysis of 348 New York Times Articles

Figure 4.5. Political Party Mentioned in Parent-Family Themed Articles by Year.

Partisanship, Ideology, and the
Portrayal of Parents in the News Media

Finally, we wanted to use the articles to assess how parents were portrayed politically within the news media. For example, have most articles assumed parents to be a disproportionately Republican or Democratic voting bloc—or a group to hold conservative or liberal attitudes? In the following chapter we explore the actual politics of parents—their partisanship, ideology, as well as their political attitudes—and compare this empirical reality with media portrayals of the politics of parenthood. To assess how the politics of parents were portrayed, we coded each article for partisanship based on whether it described or implied that parents/families were Democratic, Republican, swing voters, or made no clear reference to their political leanings. We also coded each article on whether it implied parents/families were liberal, conservative, moderate, or made no implications concerning ideology.

Turning first to the news media portrayal of the partisanship of parents, we find that the majority of articles, more than 70 percent, do in fact offer a description of the partisan leanings of parents/families. Therefore the news media are sending out strong cues to both political elites and the electorate about the political predispositions of parents. Figure 4.6 illustrates the results of those articles that include some type of partisan description or inference for each election cycle. The most pronounced trend in the partisan portrayal of parents shown in figure 4.6 is the significant increase in the number and proportion of articles portraying parents as swing voters. In 1988, for the first time, stories portraying parents as swing voters exceed all other types of portrayals. In 2004, a full 56 percent of parent/family themed election stories portrayed parents as swing voters, compared to only 11 percent portraying parents as Democrats and 14 percent as Republicans. This trend continued in 2008, with 68 percent of articles portraying parents as swing voters, while 32 percent portrayed parents as Republicans and no articles describing parents as Democrats. This means that over the last half century, and especially since the 1980s, not only have the number of presidential election stories focusing on parents and families dramatically increased, but parents have increasingly been portrayed in these stories as pivotal swing voters. The media's decision to portray parents as swing voters is significant as it heightens their attractiveness as targets for politicians and contributes to a feedback effect. The more parents are portrayed as a pivotal group of swing voters, the more the parties and the candidates try to appeal to these groups. And the more candidates appeal to parties and families, the more the media embraces the "parents as swing voters" theme in their election coverage.

The media's portrayal of the ideology of parents and families is slightly different than their partisan portrayal, as revealed in figure 4.7. Since the politicization of parenthood begins in earnest in the 1980s, in every election year except 1996 and 2000, parents are portrayed as a decidedly conservative bloc of voters. Much of the media coverage in 1996 and 2000 focused on "Soccer Moms" and implied that parents in the suburbs were tempted to vote Democratic by the party's more robust support of government action to provide health care, help the elderly, and protect the environment. In other years though, the default portrayal appears

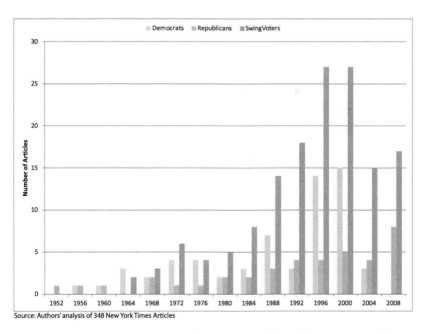

Source: Authors' analysis of 348 New York Times Articles

Figure 4.6. Media Portrayals of the Partisanship of Parents-Families.

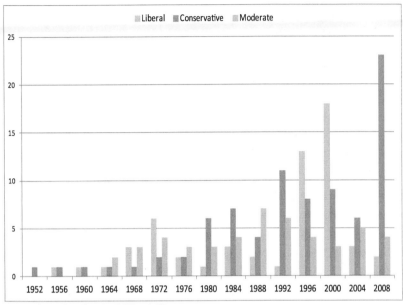

Source: Authors' analysis of 348 New York Times Articles

Figure 4.7. Media Portrayals of the Ideology of Parents-Families Over Time.

to be one where parents are a conservative group—although one that has the potential to be wooed by either party if the party embraces conservative positions on issues. Nowhere is this trend more obvious than in 2008 when Sarah Palin's presence on the Republican ticket led to many news stories discussing the strong appeal of her conservative values for American families.

The News Media and the Politics of Parenthood

The analyses of news coverage reveals how fundamental issues of parenthood and the family have become to contemporary electoral and party politics in the United States. This chapter documents that the media have politicized parenthood and the family in three important ways: First, the media has increasingly relied on parenthood and the family as a way of making sense of election events and as a means of communicating what they believe is at stake in policy disputes and election outcomes. Secondly, the media has increasingly used parents and families as a lens through which to discuss a wide range of issues, including the most pertinent and pressing issues during each electoral cycle. The increased emphasis on parenthood and family by the news media, especially in conjunction with a parallel trend among partisan elites, has the potential to prime people to think about their parental and familial roles and concerns when considering political issues and when deciding which party or candidate to support (Krosnick and Kinder 1990; Mendelsohn 1996; Nelson and Oxley 1999; Terkildsen and Schnell 1997). It is to this very topic, the political attitudes and vote choice of parents, that we turn in the next chapter. Finally, the media have increasingly portrayed parents as pivotal swing voters, albeit a bloc with conservative leanings, which heightens their attractiveness as targets for politicians and shapes the appeals of the parties—and thus furthering the politicization of parents.

We argue that the politicization of parenthood in the news media is being driven by several intertwined factors. First, the news media is being driven by political elites. As the parties and their presidential candidates increasingly used the language of the family to frame their campaign messages and their policy proposals, they have driven greater media attention to such terms and topics. Second, the politicization of parenthood by the news media is being driven by the significant changes to the family outlined in chapter 2 combined with the changing news environment. Stories about "Soccer Moms" or "Hockey Moms" tap into society's increased concern about the health of the American family and the changing role of mothers, while providing an appealing way to make sense of the multitude of campaign events that occur across the general election. "Security Mom" and "NASCAR Dad" stories also provide an attractive "hook" or vantage point from which to assess the policy proposals the candidates' put forth (Carroll 1999, 2007). Parent-family frames make for relatively quick, easy, and catchy stories, by requiring minimal investigation and reporting, while offering a human interest angle on the election. Such stories are increasingly attractive in today's news environment, which is characterized by reduced news staffs pressured to produce attractive election coverage in short amounts of time (Graber 2006, 89; Patterson 1994). Therefore, the increasing media usage of these parent-family frames reinforces and is reinforced by political actors, but also serves the increased commercialization of news values.

Finally, the politicization of parenthood and the news media is consequential because the news media have the power to shape the attitudes and the behavior of both political elites and the electorate. The media are the central way citizens, as well as political elites, acquire information about the political world. Therefore the themes the media adopt in their coverage and the way they portray or *mis*portray various groups in the electorate, such as parents, can have significant consequences. For example, the news media has increasingly portrayed parents as a pivotal bloc of voters with conservative leanings. But, as we discuss in the next chapter, parents are a diverse group and the swing voter label does not do justice to their complexities. Moreover, on some issues, parents are a distinctively liberal bloc. More accurate coverage of the politics of parents would frame electoral choices in a very different way, a possibility we explore in more depth in our concluding chapter.

5

The Political Attitudes of
Mothers and Fathers

In this chapter we examine the politics of parents—their political attitudes on major policy issues as well as their partisanship, ideology, and vote choice—over the last several decades as the context of parenting has undergone significant changes and as parenthood and the family have emerged as prominent themes in political discourse and election news coverage. Despite the significant politicization of parenthood by the parties, and the media's fascination with the politics of "NASCAR Dads" and "Security Moms," prior social science research has surprisingly little to say on whether and how parenthood is a significant adult political socialization experience. The reality is that the news media and the parties have assumed that parents are a distinctive group in the American electorate based on very little or no empirical data. In this chapter we fill in that gap, and provide a full, empirically supported portrait of the politics of mothers and fathers. More specifically, we track the attitudes of parents on major policy issues including government spending and services, national defense, and abortion over the last several decades as well as examining trends in their voting behavior and partisanship.

This chapter addresses several related questions. Over the past several decades have parents been different than their peers without children in terms of their policy attitudes, partisanship, or vote choice? Are women and men influenced by parenthood in similar or different ways? Given the different roles and societal expectations for male and female parents there are strong reasons to suspect parenthood effects may be mediated by gender. Finally, are parents distinctive in the ways the news media portrays them to be in their election reporting? In other words, are parents a conservative-leaning bloc of swing voters?

Theoretical Framework for Parenting Effects

Psychologists, sociologists, and family studies experts have empirically documented what most intuitively know to be the case: that becoming a parent is associated with profound changes in one's daily life routine, self-conception, and lens through which one views the world. Parenthood entails having less free time, dealing with tighter finances, and changing how and with whom one socializes (Gallagher and Gerstel 2001; Munch, McPherson, and Smith-Lovin 1997). Additionally, having a child brings about a salient new social role as a mother or father, a role that brings with it considerable responsibilities, worries, and psychological demands, yet also great rewards and joys. Parenthood has been shown to have an effect on parents' well-being, level of stress, and overall outlook on life (McLanahan and Adams 1987; Nomaguchi and Milkie 2003). Put simply, existing research documents that "You think differently when you have kids" (Barnes 1992, 50).

This chapter extends the work of sociologists and psychologists into the realm of politics by systematically examining whether parenthood has been associated with distinctive political attitudes, partisanship, and voting trends over the past several decades. We argue that parenthood represents a significant and underexplored agent of adult political socialization. In contrast to earlier thinking that political attitudes harden in young adulthood, political scientists now agree that attitudes can and often do change throughout the life cycle. Studies have documented attitudinal changes associated with key adult experiences such as joining the workforce, getting married, growing older, and retiring (e.g., Andersen and Cook 1985; Jennings and Stoker 2000; Pedersen 1976; Weisberg 1987). It seems reasonable to suppose that parenthood would rival, if not surpass, these other adult socialization experiences in its potential to bring about changes in adults' political outlooks. Yet while a number of studies within the socialization literature have examined the impact of having children on the level and type of political *participation* among adults (Burns, Schlozman, and Verba 1997, 2001; Jennings 1979; Sapiro 1982, 1983), very little research has been done exploring the impact of having and raising children on political *attitudes*.

We believe that raising a child has the potential to bring about distinctive attitudes on a very broad range of issues. At the most basic level, socialization theory suggests that parents will have a unique perspective on social welfare issues including those that directly or indirectly affect children's lives and well-being. As parents worry about, care for, and interact with their children, there is reason to suspect they will become increasingly concerned with policies affecting children's lives such as education, child care, and health care, as well as the overall role of government in providing programs and services. The new social role and identity mothers and fathers take on as protector and care-giver of children may also bring about changes in the way parents view issues from national security and gun control to the environment and abortion. The fact that both the parties and the news media have increasingly relied on the language of parenthood and the family to discuss a wide range of important policy issues, from the appropriate role of government to the Iraq War, is another reason we were intrigued to explore parenthood effects on a broad range of issues. In other words, the politicization of parenthood by the parties and the news media may be priming Americans to invoke their parental identities when thinking about the issues and choices at play in contemporary elections.

Additionally, socialization theory leads us to expect that parenthood will affect men and women differently. Recent studies show that in the aggregate women and men continue to play significantly different roles in the parenting process, roles shaped by gendered societal expectations for mothers and fathers. Given the different ways men and women experience and respond to parenthood, we hypothesize that parenthood effects will be mediated by gender. Since women are more involved in the parenting process, parenthood effects should be greater for women than men, especially on issues where mothers are most involved and responsible on a day-to-day basis such as education, health care, and child care. Moreover, parenthood may push the attitudes of women and men in different ideological directions. For example, mothers struggling to balance work along with primary care of their children may appreciate a more robust role of government in providing after school programs, health care, and other services. Meanwhile, given their assumed responsibilities to provide economically for their families, fathers may have reason to embrace more conservative economic and social welfare policies. Although an expanded social welfare state may potentially ease the burden on their working wives, husbands and fathers may view generous social welfare programs as leading to higher taxes and therefore undermining their ability to provide for their families economically (Iversen and Rosenbluth 2006).

The Political Attitudes of Parents: Data, Analysis, and Definitions

To understand the political impact of parenthood as comprehensively as possible we rely on data from both the General Social Survey (GSS) and the American National Election Studies (NES). Using two well-established data sets provides greater analytical power and greater confidence in uncovering trends in the relationship of parenthood and political attitudes. For practical reasons our trend analyses begin in 1972, the year that the General Social Survey began and the year the NES implemented the seven-point scales that form the basis for most of their political attitude measures. We also include a few other issues in our analyses such as attitudes about government spending on day care, defense, and environmental issues despite the fact that they were only measured in recent years. Across these two data sets we concentrate on using the most valid indicators of political attitudes across three central issue domains: the appropriate role of government in providing a social safety net; defense and security issues; and cultural values issues; as well as partisanship, ideology, and vote choice.

For the first policy domain—the appropriate role of government in providing a social safety net, which we also refer to as social welfare issues—we employed GSS data on government spending on welfare, aid to African Americans, health care, education, child care, and the environment. From NES, we employed their seven-point issue variables on the role of government in providing health care, the role of government in providing jobs and a good standard of living, whether or not the government should provide assistance to African Americans, and whether government should provide more services (1980 onward only).

Turning to national security and defense issues, we used the NES seven-point issue variable for defense spending. Since this variable was not measured prior to 1980, we also included a feeling thermometer toward the military, which was asked for a longer time period. We drew on GSS for their question concerning spending on military, defense, and armaments as well as a question concerning government spending on foreign aid.

To assess cultural values issues we used the NES seven-point measure for women's role, the feeling thermometer toward gays and lesbians, and a four-point measure of attitudes toward gays in the military that began to be asked in 1992. From the GSS we employed questions on attitudes toward homosexuality, the number of situations in which abortion should be legal, the legalization of marijuana, as well as support for gun control and the death penalty. Beyond the three policy domains we also explored the ideology, partisanship, and vote choice of parents. For ease of interpretation, every variable was coded such that higher values indicate more conservative beliefs (e.g., more spending on government services is liberal but more spending on defense is conservative) and more Republican partisanship/vote choice. Complete details on all variables can be found in appendix 2.

Given our expectations for the different effect of parenthood on men and women, we structure our analyses by breaking down survey respondents into four basic parent categories: women with children under eighteen in the home, women without children under eighteen in the home, men with children under eighteen in the home, and men without children under eighteen in the home. We follow the Census Bureau and the majority of academic studies containing a parental status variable by defining parents as those with children under eighteen living in the home, and referring to those without children under eighteen in the home as non-parents. Although this is the standard way to operationalize parenthood, it is important to note the limitations. Neither NES or GSS include a question that specifically asks whether a respondent living with a child under eighteen in the household is the custodial parent of the child. They simply record household composition rather than the actual relationship between household members.[1] To the degree that this error affects our results, it should understate the impact of parenthood and therefore not significantly alter our conclusions where there are clear effects. It is also worth noting that our measure captures all parents regardless of sexual orientation, thus both heterosexual and gay parents are included.

In an effort to summarize this large amount of data in a way that allows us to look parsimoniously for parental effects and historical patterns, we employ two different types of analyses. Our first set of analyses looks at motherhood and fatherhood effects on each issue in our three policy domains by decade. More specifically, we created mean values on all the policy issues and political variables discussed previously for parents and non-parents (separated by gender) within a particular decade, for example, all GSS surveys between 1972 and 1979. Significant differences within genders are bolded in the tables, and higher numbers indicate more conservative attitudes. These decade-by-decade results are presented in tables 5.1 through 5.4. Since these four tables contain a lot of information, we also provide a summary chart, table 5.5, which provides a simple, clear overview of motherhood and fatherhood effects across the time period of our study.

Additionally, on a handful of important issues, we trace the mean political attitudes of the four gender/parent categories during every national election across our time line. For example, the first of these figures (figure 5.1) traces the mean attitudes of female parents versus female non-parents on the issue of education spending from 1972 through the present, while its companion figure (figure 5.2) traces the same information for male parents versus male non-parents. We computed t-tests within genders for each year and issue, comparing women with children to those without, and men with children to those without. In those years where there were significant differences, we indicate this in our figures. These results are presented in figures 5.1 through 5.13.

Parenthood and Social Welfare Issues

There are several reasons to suspect that parenthood, especially motherhood, would be associated with distinctive attitudes on social welfare issues. A prominent vein of feminist theory posits that motherhood and the act of caring for and nurturing children fosters a more compassionate worldview and translates into more liberal views on a range of social welfare policies (Elshtain 1983, 1985; Ruddick 1989; Sapiro 1983). Along the same lines, much of the scholarship on the gender gap has hypothesized that the modest but long-standing gender gap on social welfare issues is, in part, the product of women's experience as mothers, driven presumably by the liberalizing impact of the motherhood experience (Andersen 1996; Deitch 1988; Piven 1985; Welch and Hibbing 1992). Finally, the analysis of elite political rhetoric presented in chapter 3 showed that the parties have increasingly wrapped their core governing philosophies about the appropriate role of government in family-friendly language, an emphasis echoed in the news media. The fact that both parties and the news media are using parents, families, and children as frames for their discussion of social welfare issues provides yet another reason to suspect parents may develop unique views on these issues.

We turn first to our results about mothers. Are mothers distinctive from non-mothers in their social welfare political attitudes? The decade-by-decade results in table 5.1 offer strong support for the idea that being a mother fosters more liberal or compassionate political attitudes, not just on issues closely connected with children such as government spending on child care and education, but on a wide range of role of government issues. Mothers are significantly more liberal than non-mothers (higher scores are more conservative in all of the tables) on almost every one of our measures of social welfare attitudes: spending/services, government jobs, welfare, aid to African Americans, spending on health care, and spending on the environment; and these effects are significant across the majority of decades. The consistency of the liberal motherhood effects documented is quite compelling. The only social welfare variable we examined with no motherhood effects was the NES measure of the role of government in providing health care, although mothers were significantly more liberal on the GSS health care variable. It is important to note that on no social welfare issues, in any decade, are mothers more conservative. On the whole, table 5.1 suggests that in contemporary America, the social welfare politics of motherhood are a distinctively liberal politics. On the whole mothers like the idea of government

Table 5.1. Bivariate Comparisons of Parenthood, Gender, and Social Welfare Attitudes by Decade

		Female without children	Female with children	Male without children	Male with children
Spending/services	NES 1980s	**3.82**	**3.53**	4.04	4.06
	NES 1990s	**3.68**	**3.28**	3.96	4.07
	NES 2000s	**3.41**	**3.21**	3.76	3.92
Government jobs	NES 1970s	4.33	4.29	**4.57**	**4.77**
	NES 1980s	**4.31**	**3.98**	4.50	4.50
	NES 1990s	**4.15**	**3.69**	4.45	4.32
	NES 2000s	**4.26**	**4.02**	4.61	4.54
Welfare	GSS 1970s	**2.37**	**2.31**	**2.36**	**2.45**
	GSS 1980s	**1.95**	**1.86**	**1.99**	**2.04**
	GSS 1990s	**1.94**	**1.84**	1.96	1.99
	GSS 2000s	**1.77**	**1.69**	1.81	1.82
Aid to blacks	GSS 1970s	**1.95**	**1.89**	**1.98**	**2.03**
	GSS 1980s	**1.85**	**1.80**	**1.90**	**1.96**
	GSS 1990s	**1.89**	**1.80**	1.95	1.96
	GSS 2000s	1.82	1.80	1.92	1.95
	NES 1970s	4.26	4.21	**4.35**	**4.51**
	NES 1980s	**4.34**	**4.21**	**4.43**	**4.55**
	NES 1990s	**4.43**	**4.27**	**4.62**	**4.79**
	NES 2000s	4.65	4.66	**4.78**	**4.98**
Health care	GSS 1970s	**1.45**	**1.40**	1.45	1.44
	GSS 1980s	**1.42**	**1.36**	1.48	1.45
	GSS 1990s	**1.36**	**1.32**	1.45	1.47
	GSS 2000s	1.26	1.27	1.37	1.38
Health care	NES 1970s	3.87	3.89	3.85	4.13
	NES 1980s	3.74	3.78	4.03	4.07
	NES 1990s	3.44	3.29	3.49	3.86
	NES 2000s	3.60	3.50	3.79	3.92
Education	GSS 1970s	**1.62**	**1.49**	1.63	1.60
	GSS 1980s	**1.45**	**1.31**	**1.47**	**1.37**
	GSS 1990s	**1.34**	**1.24**	**1.38**	**1.31**
	GSS 2000s	**1.29**	**1.22**	**1.38**	**1.29**

Child care	GSS 2000s	**1.46**	**1.38**	**1.56**	**1.51**
Environment	GSS 1970s	**1.53**	**1.45**	1.54	1.55
	GSS 1980s	**1.48**	**1.40**	1.49	1.47
	GSS 1990s	**1.46**	**1.35**	1.46	1.44
	GSS 2000s	1.41	1.39	1.46	1.45

Cell entries are mean values; higher numbers indicate more conservative attitudes. Bold cells indicate significant difference *within* gender at p<.05.

being more active to help others and providing a generous social safety net.

Figures 5.1, 5.3, and 5.5 present the same story of liberal motherhood effects, but in more detail. Figure 5.1 illustrates the attitudes of mothers and non-mothers on the issue of government spending on education over the last three decades. The figure shows that mothers have been consistently and significantly more liberal than their non-parent counterparts. (Once again, high scores equal more conservative views in this and all graphs.) Although the size of the parenthood effects are modest, t-tests show that the differences are statistically significant every year. Figure 5.3 shows that mothers have been more liberal than women without children on the issue of whether government should see to it that people receive a job and a decent standard of living in every year from 1972 to 2008. These differences reach statistical significance in eight of the years. Figure 5.5 shows that in every year the question was asked, mothers are more liberal than women without children on the issue of whether the government should provide more services even if it means an increase in spending, and this motherhood gap is also statistically significant in the majority of years. Taken together, the decade analyses as well as the more detailed year-by-year analyses tell a consistent story about the politics of motherhood. Mothers are a distinctively liberal political group, a finding consistent with theories positing that the act of raising and nurturing children fosters appreciation for a more robust social welfare state.

In contrast to women, parenthood is not as frequently associated with distinctive social welfare attitudes for men. Interestingly though, when there is a fatherhood gap on this set of issues,

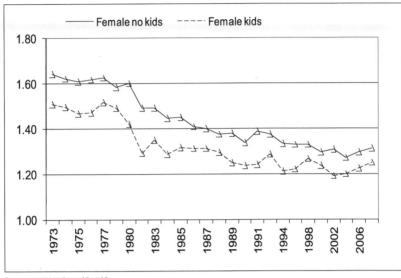

Source: 1972-2008 General Social Survey
Note: Dependent variable runs from 1-3, with higher numbers more conservative
Note: Data points with Δ indicate statistically significant differences at p<.05.

Figure 5.1. Educating Spending by Parenthood (Women Only).

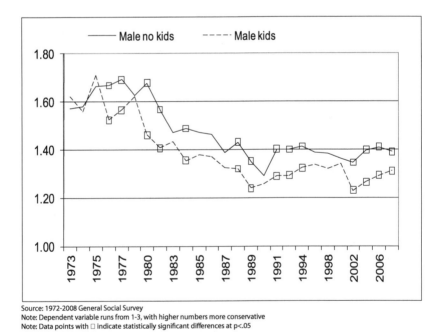

Source: 1972-2008 General Social Survey
Note: Dependent variable runs from 1-3, with higher numbers more conservative
Note: Data points with □ indicate statistically significant differences at p<.05

Figure 5.2. Educating Spending by Parenthood (Men Only).

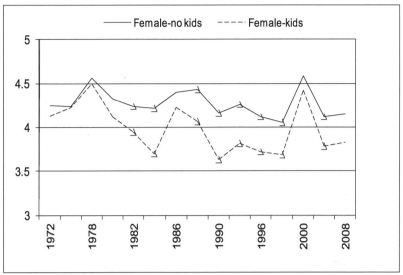

Source: 1972-2008 National Election Studies cumulative file
Note: Dependent variable runs from 1-7, with higher numbers more conservative
Note: Data points with Δ indicate statistically significant differences at p<.05.

Figure 5.3. Jobs / Standard of Living by Parenthood (Women Only).

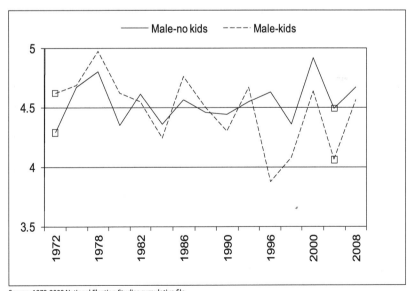

Source: 1972-2008 National Election Studies cumulative file
Note: Dependent variable runs from 1-7, with higher numbers more conservative
Note: Data points with □ indicate statistically significant differences at p<.05

Figure 5.4. Jobs / Standard of Living by Parenthood (Men Only).

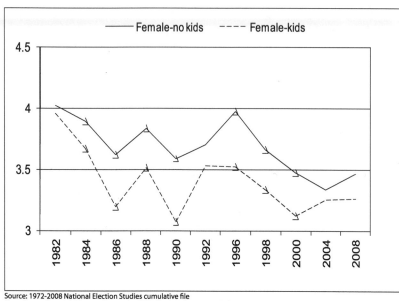

Source: 1972-2008 National Election Studies cumulative file
Note: Dependent variable runs from 1-7, with higher numbers more conservative
Note: Data points with Δ indicate statistically significant differences at p<.05.

Figure 5.5. Government Services by Parenthood (Women Only).

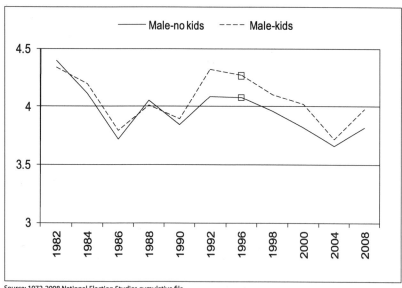

Source: 1972-2008 National Election Studies cumulative file
Note: Dependent variable runs from 1-7, with higher numbers more conservative
Note: Data points with ☐ indicate statistically significant differences at p<.05.

Figure 5.6. Government Services by Parenthood (Men Only).

in most cases, fathers are more conservative than men without children. In other words, parenthood appears to push men and women in opposite ideological directions in the social welfare realm. Table 5.1, the decade-by-decade table, shows that fathers are significantly more conservative than non-fathers in one or more decades on the issue of government providing jobs, government assistance to the poor, and government assistance to African Americans. Figures 5.4 and 5.6 show that starting around the early to mid-1990s fathers are consistently more conservative on the issue of government providing jobs and a decent standard of living as well as the issue of government services and spending then men with no children, although these differences only reach the level of statistical significance in one year in each figure. These results suggest that fathers view a generous social welfare state as a negative, perhaps as an intrusion on their ability to economically provide for their families. This makes sense especially given studies showing that fathers respond to parenthood by working even more hours outside the home.

It is also important to point out that on two social welfare issues, education and child care, fathers are actually more liberal than their non-parent counterparts (table 5.2 and figure 5.2). Perhaps because these two issues are most closely connected with children, fathers do not see them as connected to an overall broadening of government's role, and fathers view more government spending in these areas as directly benefitting themselves. Thus on education and child care parenthood is associated with liberal effects for both men and women, but on all other social welfare issues, parenthood appears to push mothers and fathers in opposite directions.

Parenthood, Defense, and the Military

Scholars and media pundits alike have long speculated about the impact of parenthood, especially motherhood, on political attitudes concerning war. Some feminist scholars have argued that mothers possess more antimilitaristic attitudes because of their unique role in having and raising children (Elshtain 1981, 1983, 1985, 1987; Ruddick 1989). One of the most prominent scholars to articulate this position, Sara Ruddick, has argued that "Out of maternal practice a distinctive kind of thinking arises that is incompatible with military strategy but consonant with pacifist commitment to non-violence" (Ruddick 1983, 233). Yet, in the wake of the 9-11 terrorist attacks, a different image of the relationship between military/war issues and parenthood emerged in news coverage. "Security Mom," and to a lesser extent "NASCAR Dad," stories portrayed parents as being distinctively conservative on defense and security issues as a direct result of their role as protectors of their children (Elder and Greene 2007).

Our results, presented in table 5.2 and figure 5.7 provide modest support for the "maternal thinking" theory that motherhood is associated with more pacifist views, and strongly reject the "Security Mom" hypothesis. The decade-by-decade results (table

Table 5.2. Bivariate Comparisons of Parenthood, Gender, and Defense / Foreign Policy Attitudes by Decade

		Female without children	Female with children	Male without children	Male with children
Defense spending	NES 1980s	4.02	3.95	4.20	4.41
	NES 1990s	3.57	3.59	3.59	3.67
	NES 2000s	4.30	4.30	4.64	4.62
	GSS 1970s	**1.92**	**1.87**	1.91	1.94
	GSS 1980s	1.88	1.85	1.87	1.94
	GSS 1990s	**1.83**	**1.80**	1.95	1.96
	GSS 2000s	**2.02**	**1.94**	1.99	2.00
Military Feeling	NES 1970	**71.31**	**68.33**	**65.53**	**68.71**
Thermometer	NES 1980s	67.75	67.83	**65.41**	**69.13**
	NES 1990s	69.95	70.40	68.93	70.31
	NES 2000s	75.58	76.15	76.23	76.31
Foreign aid	GSS 1970s	2.70	2.70	2.71	2.79
	GSS 1980s	**2.70**	**2.62**	**2.69**	**2.73**
	GSS 1990s	2.69	2.67	2.68	2.71
	GSS 2000s	2.56	2.54	**2.57**	**2.61**

Cell entries are mean values; higher numbers indicate more conservative attitudes. Bold cells indicate significant difference *within* gender at p<.05.

5.2) reveal that when mothers are distinctive from women without children in the home, the motherhood effects are in a liberal direction, just like in the social welfare policy realm. In the 1970s, mothers as a group were significantly "less warm" toward the military than their non-mother counterparts. In the 1980s, mothers were significantly more supportive of increased spending on foreign aid. And, in the 1990s as well as the first decade of the twenty-first century, mothers were significantly less supportive of government spending on the military, armaments, and defense than non-mothers. In the year-by-year comparison of the attitudes of mothers versus non-mothers on defense spending presented in figure 5.7, mothers were significantly different than non-mothers in five of those years; each time mothers held more liberal views and were less supportive of spending on the military. It is also important to point out that in no cases are mothers more conservative than non-mothers, suggesting that the "Security Mom" label truly has no basis in empirical reality.

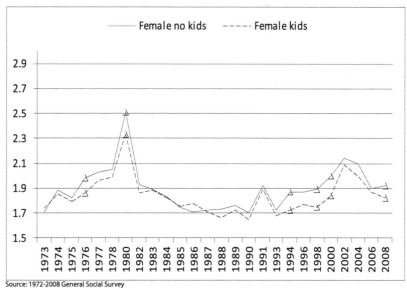

Source: 1972-2008 General Social Survey
Note: Dependent variable runs from 1-3, with higher numbers more conservative
Note: Data points with Δ indicate statistically significant differences at p<.05.

Figure 5.7. Defense Spending by Parenthood (Women Only).

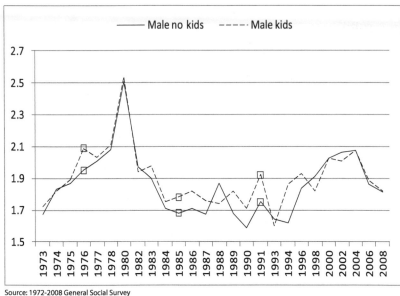

Source: 1972-2008 General Social Survey
Note: Dependent variable runs from 1-3, with higher numbers more conservative
Note: Data points with □ indicate statistically significant differences at p<.05

Figure 5.8. Defense Spending by Parenthood (Men Only).

For men, however, the impact of parenthood in the defense/ military policy realm is in the opposite ideological direction. Fathers hold more conservative attitudes on issues concerning defense and foreign policy, and these differences reach statistical significance in several decades as shown in table 5.2. Figure 5.8, which charts the views of fathers and non-fathers on the issue of government spending on the military over time, shows that in the majority of years male parents and non-parents do not hold significantly different attitudes, yet in each of the three years that fathers are unique their attitudes are more conservative than men without children.

Taken together we see that, while modest, the parenthood effects that do appear in the defense/military issue domain push mothers and fathers further apart ideologically. Our results are consistent with the idea that motherhood fosters pacifist attitudes on military and defense issues. Fathers, in contrast, are either no different than their counterparts without children, or respond to parenthood by seeking a stronger military to defend the nation and presumably their families.

Parents and Cultural Values Issues

Conventional wisdom, as well as a number of stories in the news, imply that parents are a distinctively conservative group, especially on "family values" issues. Our results indicate that this is not the case, at least for women. What is perhaps most notable about the effects of motherhood on cultural values attitudes is the lack of an effect. The one cultural values issue that shows consistent motherhood effects is the appropriate role for women in society, and on this issue, mothers are significantly more liberal than women without children in every decade (table 5.3). The other three significant effects for women in table 5.3 show a fairly mixed picture. In the 1980s mothers are slightly more liberal on the issue of legalizing marijuana, while in the 1990s mothers are slightly more conservative. Also, in the most recent decade mothers are more conservative than non-mothers on the issue of abortion. Figure 5.9 shows that in most years mothers and non-mothers are no different on the issue of abortion, but in three years mothers are significantly more conservative. Given conventional wisdom that parents are more conservative on cultural values type issues, it is interesting to note that table 5.3 shows that female parents and non-parents do not differ in their attitudes on same-sex relations or attitudes toward gays and lesbians.

Turning to men, we see that there are actually more, and more consistent, fatherhood effects than motherhood effects in this policy realm. The issue of abortion is characterized by some of the most consistent, conservative fatherhood effects. Table 5.3 shows that the conservative impact of fatherhood on abortion attitudes is statistically significant in all four decades examined. Similarly, figure 5.10 shows a consistent conservative fatherhood effect on abortion that is significant in eleven of the years examined. This same pattern of conservative fatherhood effects characterizes all the other cultural values type issues we examined. Fathers are more conservative on the issue of same-sex relations asked on GSS and on the feeling thermometer question about gays/lesbians asked on NES, differences which reach statistical significance

Table 5.3. Bivariate Comparisons of Parenthood, Gender, and Cultural Values Issues by Decade

		Female without children	Female with children	Male without children	Male with children
Women's role	NES 1970s	**3.82**	**3.48**	3.52	3.52
	NES 1980s	**3.39**	**3.02**	3.28	3.30
	NES 1990s	**2.71**	**2.40**	2.58	2.60
	NES 2000s	**1.90**	**1.75**	1.99	2.02
Homosexuality	GSS 1970s	3.39	3.36	**3.31**	**3.43**
	GSS 1980s	3.42	3.39	**3.38**	**3.51**
	GSS 1990s	3.07	3.06	3.15	3.26
	GSS 2000s	2.77	2.78	2.88	2.98
Gays/lesbians	NES 1980s	68.50	68.91	**71.31**	**76.61**
Feeling	NES 1990s	53.41	52.73	61.68	64.74
Thermometer	NES 2000s	50.89	52.09	50.57	51.57
Gays in the	NES 1990s	1.93	2.07	2.58	2.69
military	NES 2000s	1.67	1.60	2.08	2.02
Abortion	GSS 1970s	1.95	1.96	**1.71**	**2.13**
	GSS 1980s	2.13	2.25	**1.88**	**2.20**
	GSS 1990s	2.02	2.08	**1.78**	**2.17**
	GSS 2000s	**2.26**	**2.52**	2.04	2.33
Marijuana	GSS 1970s	1.78	1.80	**1.67**	**1.76**
legalization	GSS 1980s	**1.84**	**1.82**	1.74	1.78
	GSS 1990s	**1.79**	**1.81**	**1.69**	**1.74**
	GSS 2000s	1.67	1.68	1.59	1.60
Gun control	GSS 1970s	1.18	1.19	**1.32**	**1.39**
	GSS 1980s	1.20	1.21	**1.32**	**1.38**
	GSS 1990s	1.13	1.12	1.25	1.28
	GSS 2000s	1.14	1.12	1.28	1.27
Death penalty	GSS 1970s	1.64	1.63	**1.73**	**1.76**
	GSS 1980s	1.71	1.71	**1.79**	**1.83**
	GSS 1990s	1.73	1.74	1.81	1.82
	GSS 2000s	1.63	1.63	**1.72**	**1.78**

Cell entries are mean values; higher numbers indicate more conservative attitudes. Bold cells indicate significant difference *within* gender at p<.05.

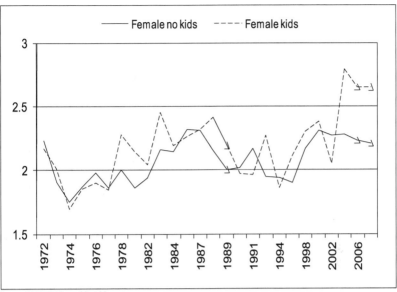

Source: 1972-2008 General Social Survey
Note: Dependent variable runs from 0-6, with higher numbers more conservative
Note: Data points with Δ indicate statistically significant differences at p<.05.

Figure 5.9. Abortion by Parenthood (Women Only).

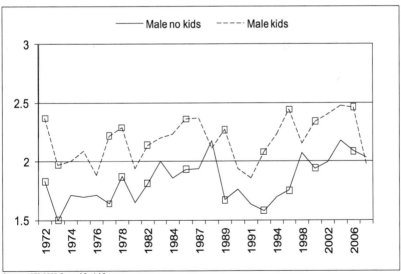

Source: 1972-2008 General Social Survey
Note: Dependent variable runs from 0-6, with higher numbers more conservative
Note: Data points with □ indicate statistically significant differences at p<.05

Figure 5.10. Abortion by Parenthood (Men Only).

in the 1970s and 1980s. In three of the four decades we examined (not the 1990s) fathers are significantly more conservative than men without children on the issue of the death penalty. And in three decades—the 1970s, 1980s, and 2000s—fathers are significantly more conservative on the issue of gun control (table 5.3).

The Partisanship, Ideology, and Vote Choice of Parents

In addition to examining parenthood effects in specific issue domains we also looked at broader political factors such as partisanship, vote choice, and ideology. Table 5.4 provides comparisons of parenthood/gender and vote choice, ideology, and partisanship by decade. This table shows that female parents and female non-parents do not display any significant differences on these variables. Similarly figure 5.11 shows that the partisanship of mothers has not been different from non-mothers in any systematic way

Table 5.4. Bivariate Comparisons of Parenthood, Gender, Vote Choice, Ideology, and Partisanship by Decade

		Female without children	Female with children	Male without children	Male with children
Ideology	NES 1970s	4.22	4.15	4.16	4.25
	NES 1980s	4.24	4.24	**4.30**	**4.44**
	NES 1990s	4.11	4.14	**4.19**	**4.44**
	NES 2000s	4.09	4.19	**4.31**	**4.52**
Party ID	NES 1970s	3.61	3.67	3.66	3.64
	NES 1980s	3.70	3.60	**3.77**	**3.97**
	NES 1990s	3.52	3.63	**3.80**	**4.02**
	NES 2000s	3.60	3.68	3.91	4.00
Republican vote	GSS 1970s	0.56	0.54	**0.53**	**0.57**
	GSS 1980s	0.50	0.48	0.53	0.56
	GSS 1990s	0.45	0.44	**0.50**	**0.60**
	GSS 2000s	0.45	0.46	**0.52**	**0.58**

Cell entries are mean values; higher numbers indicate more conservative attitudes. Bold cells indicate significant difference *within* gender at p<.05.

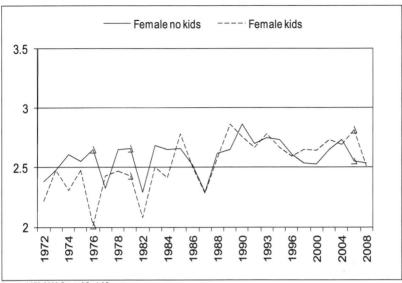

Source: 1972-2008 General Social Survey
Note: Dependent variable runs from 1-7, with higher numbers more conservative
Note: Data points with Δ indicate statistically significant differences at p<.05.

Figure 5.11. Party Identification by Parenthood (Women Only).

over the past several decades. Despite these non-findings, it is worthwhile to point out that across the past three decades, mothers—like women overall—have been significantly more liberal and more Democratic in their partisanship and vote choice than both fathers and men without children.

In contrast, fathers are significantly different than men without children in terms of ideology, partisanship, and vote choice (table 5.4). In all decades examined, fathers are more conservative in terms of ideology and in three of these decades these differences reach statistical significance. In two of four decades fathers are significantly more Republican than non-fathers in terms of their partisan identification; and in all decades fathers were more Republican in their vote choice, a difference that reached standard levels of statistical significance in three of four decades.

Figure 5.12 traces the partisanship of men parents and non-parents from 1972 through the present and shows that while men as a group have moved in a Republican direction over the last sev-

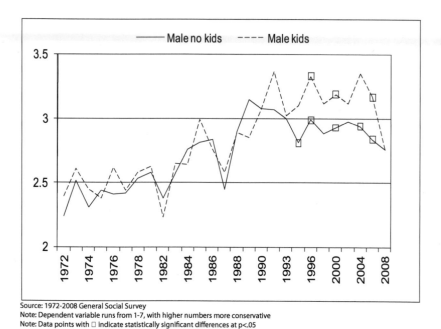

Source: 1972-2008 General Social Survey
Note: Dependent variable runs from 1-7, with higher numbers more conservative
Note: Data points with □ indicate statistically significant differences at p<.05

Figure 5.12. Party Identification by Parenthood (Men Only).

eral decades, this trend is particularly pronounced among fathers. In five of the past ten election cycles, the Republican gap between fathers and non-fathers has been statistically significant. This phenomenon of fathers becoming more Republican at a faster rate than men overall is even more clearly illustrated in figure 5.13, which includes trend lines.

On the whole, these results reveal that much of the conventional wisdom about the politics of parents is wrong. Many news stories and widely read news columns have suggested that Democrats must become more conservative in order to win over parents and win elections (e.g., Barnes 1992; Brooks 2004; Greenberg 2001; Kotkin and Frey 2004; Whitehead 2004). These stories are premised on an inaccurate or at least partially inaccurate understanding of the politics of parenthood. While fathers are distinctively conservative and distinctively Republican, characterizing parents in this manner is quite inaccurate. Mothers, like women overall, remain a liberal-leaning, Democratic voting bloc.

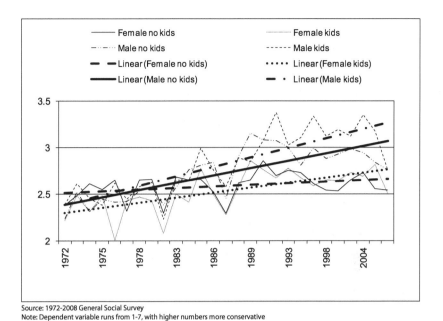

Source: 1972-2008 General Social Survey
Note: Dependent variable runs from 1-7, with higher numbers more conservative

Figure 5.13. Party Identification by Parenthood and Gender (with Trendlines).

The Politics and Polarization of Parenthood

We began this chapter by asking whether over the past several decades parents have been different than their peers without children in terms of their policy attitudes, partisanship, or vote choice. The answer is a clear yes. This chapter presents an abundance of empirical evidence, summarized in table 5.5, that parenthood is indeed political. Men and women with children in the home are significantly different than their counterparts without children on a wide range of issues, not just on issues directly related to childrearing.

We also found that for the most part women and men are influenced by parenthood in very different ways (see table 5.5). First of all, the issue domains where parenthood effects are strongest differ by gender. Motherhood effects are particularly robust

Table 5.5. Summary of Parenthood Effects, 1970–2008

	Mothers more liberal	Fathers more conservative
Spending and services	X	
Jobs	X	X
Welfare	X	X
Government aid to blacks	X	X
Health care	X	
Education	X	
Child care	X	
Environment	X	
Defense spending	X	
Women's role	X	
Homosexuality		X
Abortion		X
Marijuana legalization		X
Gun control		X
Death penalty		X
Ideology		X
Party ID		X
Vote choice		X

on social welfare/role of government issues, while fathers are distinctively conservative on cultural values issues. Second, on almost all issues, parenthood is associated with polarized ideological impacts; motherhood is associated with more liberal attitudes while fatherhood is associated with more conservative attitudes. This is particularly true on social welfare issues although liberal motherhood effects are also present on defense and to a lesser extent social issues. Parenthood effects were much smaller and on some issues nonexistent for fathers, but among the effects that did exist they tell a very consistent story, that fatherhood is associated with more conservative attitudes. Finally, the trend analysis shows that fathers and mothers have moved further apart ideologically on most political issues and in terms of partisanship over the past three decades.

The different effects of parenthood on men and women are consistent with the different roles of mothers and fathers combined with the polarized messages about parenthood articulated by the parties. Despite changes in family structure over the past several decades, mothers are still expected to be the nurturers and primary care-givers of their children, expectations which mothers continue to carry out despite their entrance into the paid workforce. Such nurturing and care-giving appears to foster a greater appreciation for programs designed to help children as well as a more liberal view of the role of government overall and more pacifist attitudes on issues concerning the military and defense. The growing number of single mothers and working mothers has pushed women into reliance on people as well as government programs to help them care for their families and appears to have politicized mothers in a liberal direction. Although the increasing use of family-friendly appeals has been bipartisan, the experience of contemporary mothers appears most in line with the messages coming from the Democratic Party and its pledge to help working families through more government regulation (e.g., mandating family leave policies, raising the minimum wage) and supporting increased funding for government programs including public education and job training.

Meanwhile fathers are still expected to be the economic providers for their families and in fact respond to becoming parents by working even more hours outside the home. Fathers appear to respond to parenthood by viewing government social welfare programs and the increased taxes they typically require as intruding on their ability to provide economically for their families. Male parents may also be "defending" their lifestyle choice of marriage and children by increasing their opposition to gay marriage and abortion. Finally, men seem to respond to parenthood by embracing a protector role—offering greater support for the military, capital punishment, and efforts to fight crime—while preserving their right to own guns without governmental intrusion. The response of fathers is right in line with the family appeals of the Republican Party that emphasize the importance of minimalist government, lower taxes, and policies supporting "traditional family values" as the best way to support and strengthen the American family.

The final question we posed at the start of this chapter was whether parents are the distinctive and critical political group that the parties assume they are and the media portray them to be? The answer to this is mostly no. The results in this chapter show that many assumptions about the politics of parents made by the news media as well as the candidates are not accurate. First, mothers are not more likely to support increases in defense spending to protect their families as the "Security Mom" label indicated. In fact, more often than not over the past several decades mothers have supported less defense spending than other women. Rather, our most consistent and substantive finding is that mothers are more likely than non-mothers, as well as men and fathers, to support a robust and generous social welfare state. Thus, more accurate media labels would be "Social Welfare Mothers."

Secondly, parents are not distinctively conservative on "family values" issues. Fatherhood is associated with conservative impacts on this set of issues for men, but this is not the case for mothers. Finally, the parent vote is not the "swing vote" that the news media has increasingly portrayed it to be. There really is no parent vote, but rather mothers and fathers form very distinct blocs of voters. Fathers are a Republican bloc, while mothers are a key part of the Democratic coalition. Thus the suggestion that the parties need to become more conservative or embrace family values proposals in order to win over the parent bloc is not accurate.

In conclusion, it is important to point out that this chapter focused solely on bivariate analysis, exploring parenthood and political attitudes. Although basic, these analyses provide a substantial amount of important information about parenthood as an agent of adult socialization. Regardless of how parenthood may correlate with other demographic factors, the fact that mothers and fathers do indeed represent distinctive political blocs is important information. Not only do the analyses presented in this chapter provide an accurate picture of the political attitudes of two much-discussed groups—mothers and fathers—but also such information is critical to the strategies of the parties and the actual playing out of American politics. In the next chapter we delve further into the politics of parenthood by employing multivariate models, which allow us to control for potentially confounding variables and better isolate and explore the political impact of parenthood.

6

Marriage, Race, and the
Politics of Parenthood

The last chapter offered empirical evidence that the personal is indeed political. Parenthood, one of the most life-changing experiences, is associated with significantly different attitudes on a wide range of important issues in multiple policy domains. The overtime analysis of political attitudes and values showed that mothers and fathers are different from their peers without children, although the ideological direction of parenthood effects varies by gender.

In this chapter, we use data from the 2008 National Election Studies to further develop and deepen our understanding of the politics of parenthood. More specifically, we use 2008 data to explore whether the motherhood and fatherhood effects documented in the previous chapter remain significant predictors of political attitudes on major policy issues as well as broader political orientations when potentially confounding factors such as age, income, education, and religion are controlled. In other words, to what extent does having and raising a child or children represent a substantive and significant political socialization experience?

We also deepen our understanding of the political impact of parenthood by taking a more extensive look at the relationship between parenthood and two potentially mediating variables: the marital status and the race/ethnicity of parents. This chapter seeks to address several interrelated questions. How does the impact of parenthood compare to the closely associated experience of marriage? Do marriage and parenthood act as reinforcing influences on the political attitudes of men and women, or do these two important life transitions act as cross-pressures? Perhaps most importantly, do the politics of parenthood vary by marital status? Additionally, given the growing racial and ethnic diversity of parents in the United States we also are interested in exploring whether the parenthood effects we find are universal for all mothers and fathers or whether they differ across racial and ethnic groups. By employing more sophisticated models that look closely at the way marital and racial status interact with parenthood we are able to present a fuller explanation of how family life shapes public opinion and vote choice in contemporary American politics.

Marriage and Parenthood

Parenthood and marriage are both major life transitions that most adults experience. Although intimately personal experiences, both the transition from being single to being married as well as the experience of having and raising children hold the potential to shape political views. Interestingly, much more scholarly research has focused on the former of these two adult experiences, marriage, than on the impact of parenthood.

A wealth of studies have focused specifically on the so-called marriage gap—the higher levels of support for Republican candidates among married than non-married voters—which first emerged in the 1972 presidential election and has characterized every presidential election since. The magnitude of the marriage gap is large, consistently bigger than the widely discussed gender gap, and has been growing. According to 2008 exit polls, married persons voted for Republican candidate John McCain by a margin of 19 percentage points over unmarried voters (52 to 33 percent).

While the Republican advantage among married voters has become a predictable characteristic of American elections, a comprehensive understanding of its cause or causes remains elusive. In his analysis of presidential elections from 1960 through 1984, Weisberg (1987) demonstrated the marriage gap was predominantly a demographics gap: married couples were more likely to be white and have higher socioeconomic status, both characteristics positively associated with support for Republicans. Only in 1972 did marriage remain a significant predictor after controlling for demographics.[1] More recent studies show that marriage significantly predicted Republican voting in multivariate models controlling for demographics in 2000 and 2004, but not 1988, 1992, 1996 (Greenberg and Berktold 2005; Tinnick 2003).

The main explanation for the non-demographic aspects of the marriage gap offered in the scholarly literature as well as the press goes like this: Those who choose to get and stay married not only have more conservative predispositions to begin with, but become more conservative/Republican because the experiences they have as married people, that is, buying a home, having children, and for some women leaving the workforce, push them in a conservative direction and because married persons are drawn to defend their decision to get and stay married in a society where such a lifestyle choice is increasingly uncommon (Gerson 1985, 1987; Greenberg 2001; Plissner 1983). All this draws married voters to the Republican Party, particularly as it increased its emphasis on family values (Arnold and Weisberg 1996).

One problem with some of these explanations for the marriage gap is that they explicitly or implicitly conflate marriage and children. This is a problem for two reasons. First, while the majority of parents are still raising children in two-parent households, these are two demographic patterns that have become increasingly unconnected. Fewer married people are having children than in previous decades, while more unmarried people have been becoming parents (Dye 2005, 11; Teachman, Tedrow, and Crowder 2000).[2] Over the last several decades about one-third of births have been to unmarried women, and today about a third of households with children under eighteen are headed by single parents (Dye 2005, 5; Fields 2004).

Moreover, conflating marriage and parenthood is problematic because theoretically and practically speaking, the impact of these two major life events are quite different. Marriage tends to enhance socioeconomic status as well as health and happiness, especially for men (Waite and Gallagher 2000), while parenthood pushes people toward financial strain, greater dependence on government assistance programs, and greater psychological stress, especially for women (Lugaila 2005; Rauch 2001). Studies have pointed out that women in particular pay a substantial motherhood wage penalty (Budig and England 2001; Waite and Gallagher 2000, 107). As a result, the political consequences of marriage and parenthood might be quite different in terms of ideological direction, especially for women. Finally, despite the greater attention the marriage gap has received in the academic literature, there are reasons to suspect that parenthood effects may rival if not surpass the effects of marriage, as parenthood arguably brings about a more profound and sustained life transition. Thus, in this chapter we seek to untangle and compare the political impact of parenthood and marriage.

Along similar lines we also seek to explore whether the impact of parenthood varies by marital status. For example, we wondered if the liberalizing impacts of motherhood, especially when it comes to social welfare issues, may be most pronounced among parents who are raising children without a spouse. For many single parents, becoming a parent has pushed them into direct reliance on government assistance programs from Medicaid to housing assistance to food assistance programs for at least some period of time. Moreover, almost by definition, single parents need to rely more heavily on people and programs outside of the traditional family to provide much of their children's care (Anderson and Vail 1999). These experiences, combined with the intensive, day-to-day caring of children as a single parent, should lead to strong appreciation of a robust role of the government in providing a social welfare safety net. Meanwhile, married parents may respond to the experience of motherhood or fatherhood by "defending" their lifestyle choice and adopting more conservative stances especially on family or cultural values issues.

Race, Ethnicity, and Parenthood

For several reasons we argue that a contemporary understanding of the role of parenthood and family structure in American politics demands a careful examination not only of marriage, but also of race as a mediating factor. One reason for this is pure demographics. Census data show that parents in the United States are an increasingly diverse group in terms of race and ethnicity. Latino, Asian, and to a lesser extent black women are having children at a higher rate than white women, making parents a more diverse group than the nation as a whole. Secondly, scholars in a range of disciplines have argued that marriage and parenthood have different meanings for blacks, Latinos, and whites (e.g., Collins 1994; Coontz 1992, chapter 10; Hill 2001; Teachman, Tedrow, and Crowder 2000). Finally, parenthood occurs in fairly different contexts for different racial and ethnic groups. Marriage has been and continues to be a much more common experience for whites than blacks and to a lesser extent Latinos.[3] African Americans are much more likely than other racial and ethnic groups to become parents outside of the institution of marriage (Dye 2005, 5).[4] Scholars argue that the lower rates of marriage and higher rates of single parenthood among black Americans are the product of several factors including historical and contemporary experiences with discrimination, the influence of non-nuclear African family structures, and the paucity of marriageable men in local markets (Collins 1994; Hill 2001). Minority parents also experience much higher rates of poverty and reliance on government assistance programs (Lugaila 2005).[5]

One of the only existing studies to explore the mediating impact of race on parental attitudes found significant differences, further emphasizing the need to examine parents across racial categories. Morgan and Waite's (1987) analysis of panel data from 1972 to 1979 found that the transition to parenthood was associated with developing more traditional orientations concerning sex roles for married white parents, but had the opposite effect, fostering more egalitarian orientations for black, non-married parents.

Data and Methods

To explore the impact of parenthood in greater depth, we focus exclusively on 2008, the most recent national election. For a number of reasons, the 2008 election represents a good case study for exploring the impacts of parenthood. Similar to presidential elections from 1992 forward, mothers and fathers were given a high-profile role in the 2008 presidential campaign by the candidates, the parties, and the news media, thus priming voters to think about their parental roles and familial concerns when considering political issues and when deciding which party or candidate to support. Presidential candidates Barack Obama and John McCain turned to the language of the family to frame their contrasting proposals for the nation's ailing economy and articulate their visions of the appropriate role of government. And in keeping with recent tradition, the news media introduced new "parent-labels" including "Hockey Moms," "Walmart Moms," and "Mortgage Moms" as lenses through which to analyze the 2008 presidential contest. Fathers and fatherhood were also a visible theme. Democratic candidate Barack Obama, in particular, devoted considerable space in his appeals to the public on the theme of "Responsible Fatherhood" and the need for fathers to become more involved in the lives of their children.[6] We rely on the 2008 American National Election Study data for our analysis in this chapter. While both NES and GSS contain a wealth of public opinion data, we utilize the NES data because it contains superior measures of the key policy attitudes and political dispositions that are most relevant to our empirical investigations in this chapter.

Similar to the previous chapter, the analyses here seek to explore the impact of motherhood and fatherhood on the same broad set of policy attitudes discussed in the previous chapter—social welfare, national security/defense, and cultural values—as well as ideology, partisanship, and vote choice, but in this chapter we employ multivariate models to control for potentially confounding variables. The first dependent variable we wanted to explore was policy attitudes on social welfare issues. Since there are so many questions tapping attitudes about social welfare and the role of government we sought to simplify our analyses by employing a social welfare index originally created by Howell and Day (2000) in their analysis of the complexities of the gender gap and used in other publications (Elder and Greene 2006). The constituent components of this social welfare index include the standard NES seven-point questions on health care, government support for jobs, and level of government services[7] as well as measures querying support for federal spending on child care, social security, welfare, aid to the poor, and public schools.[8] The three seven-point issues and five spending issues all loaded on a single factor. Following Howell and Day (2000), we created standardized values for each variable and then took the mean across these eight standardized scores to create our social welfare index, running from −1.37 to 2.07, with higher numbers more conservative.

To explore attitudes on defense and national security issues we employed two different measures: an Iraq War index and attitudes on defense spending. Since the Iraq War has been one of the dominant national security–related issues of the twenty-first century and inspired the news media to coin the term "Security Mom," we were particularly interested to explore the impact of motherhood and fatherhood on Iraq War attitudes. We created an Iraq War index composed of three items: approval for the government's handling of the war in Iraq, approval for Bush's handling of Iraq, and whether the war in Iraq was worth it. As these items loaded on a single factor, we created a single four-point Iraq War index running from 0 strong opposition to 3 strong support. In addition to the Iraq War index, we explore parenthood effects on defense spending by employing the standard NES seven-point scale variable with higher scores indicating the more conservative position of increased defense spending.

To address cultural values issues we focused on two of the most high-profile "family values" issues—the issues of abortion and gay marriage. We used the new NES abortion question, which incorporates the thoroughness of the GSS measures (six yes-no questions querying support for abortion under a variety of potential circumstances) with more nuanced nine-point response categories. The gay marriage item allowed for responses of no government recognition, civil unions, or gay marriage and runs from 1 to 3, with higher scores being more conservative. In addition to these policy realms we employ three political measures as dependent variables: Party identification measured the standard way from 0, strong Democrat to 6, strong Republican; political ideology using the standard seven-point scale running from 1, extremely liberal, to 7, extremely conservative; and finally, we included a variable for presidential vote coded 1 for a vote for McCain, 0 for an Obama vote.

The key independent variable in all of the analyses is whether or not the respondent is a parent, measured as whether the respondent has a child under eighteen living in the home with them. The other independent variables we are particularly interested in are marriage, measured as 1 presently married and 0 presently not married, and race, which we code based on respondent self-identification. Ideally, we would have liked to separate out various racial/ethnic groups, especially black Americans versus Latinos, but given other constraints on the usable number of respondents, it would not have been possible to obtain statistically meaning-ful results. We therefore simply code as white and racial/ethnic minorities.

We estimated regression models for all of our dependent variables controlling for a range of demographic and political fac-tors that are correlated with parenthood and could thus poten-tially explain parent differences found in the previous chapter. The control variables include age, income, education, religiosity, employment status, region (South or not), partisanship, as well as marriage and race as discussed.[9] The coding for all of these variables can be found in appendix 3.

Because there are strong theoretical reasons to suspect par-enthood would impact men and women differently, an expectation borne out in the previous chapter, we estimated separate models for men and women.[10] To explore how marriage and race might mediate the impact of parenthood, we also estimated a series of models including interaction terms for marital status-parenthood and race-parenthood. Since very few of the interaction terms we estimated proved to have statistical significance or to alter in any meaningful way the interpretation of the rest of the model, we did not create additional tables, but rather discuss the significant and non-significant interaction terms in our discussion of results where appropriate.

Results: Parenthood, Marriage, Race, and Social Welfare Attitudes

In the previous chapter we found that motherhood was consistent-ly associated with more liberal attitudes on social welfare issues over the past several decades. Our analysis of 2008 data also con-firms this liberal motherhood effect. The multivariate regression results shown in table 6.1 lend further support for the idea that there is something about being a mother that promotes more lib-eral attitudes on social welfare issues. Women with children in the home are substantively and significantly more likely than their non-mother counterparts to support the government playing an active role in providing programs and services to its citizens, even when a full range of potentially confounding variables, such as partisanship, age, income, and religiosity are controlled. Consis-

Table 6.1. Social Welfare Attitudes by Parenthood with
Demographic Controls

	Women only	Men only
Parent	–.116**	.123*
	(.044)	(.051)
Married	.026	.019
	(.042)	(.051)
Age	.003**	.003*
	(.001)	(.002)
Income	.011**	.009*
	(.004)	(.004)
Education	.003	.015
	(.009)	(.009)
Religiosity	.053**	.020
	(.017)	(.018)
Employed	.015	.022
	(.046)	(.053)
South	.044	.118**
	(.039)	(.042)
Minority	.088+	.134*
	(.048)	(.054)
Party ID	.106**	.109**
	(.010)	(.011)
N	538	500
R^2	.275	.276

Source: 2008 NES Data.

** p<.01, * p<.05, + p<.10, two-tailed tests.

Note: Cell entries in columns one and two are unstandardized OLS coefficients. Standard errors are in parentheses.

tent with some feminist theories, there seems to be something about the experience of being a mother that leads to more liberal social welfare attitudes (Ruddick 1980, 1989; Sapiro 1983).

Given the greater attention marriage has received over parenthood in the academic literature it is interesting to note that marriage, unlike motherhood, has no significant impact on the social welfare attitudes of women. Additionally, we ran alternative versions of our regression model including a marriage-motherhood interaction, to see if the effect of parenthood was particularly pronounced among unmarried or married women, and the interaction did not yield significant results. This non-finding once again underscores the universality of the liberal motherhood effects.

Finally, we were also interested in exploring the impact of parenthood across racial and ethnic groups. To explore the mediating role of race we added a motherhood-minority status interaction to our model presented in table 6.1 and found that the interaction term was statistically significant and the coefficient was positive. What this means is that parenthood has a greater liberalizing impact for white women than for women who are members of racial and ethnic minority groups. This makes sense as black and Latino women are already distinctively liberal on social welfare issues, thus motherhood moves white mothers even further in the liberal direction in comparison.

In the previous chapter we found that parenthood was not as frequently associated with distinctive social welfare attitudes for men as for women, but that when there was a fatherhood gap, in most cases fathers were more conservative than men without children. The conservative impact of fatherhood is strongly supported in our regression results (table 6.1). Being a father is strongly and significantly associated with conservative views on social welfare issues. We thought the impact of parenthood on the social welfare attitudes might be weaker for men given that female parents remain much more involved in caring for children and tending to the day-to-day health care, education, day care, and nurturing needs than male parents, but this was not the case. Parenthood strongly shapes the social welfare attitudes of both men and women, only in opposite ideological directions.

In the previous chapter we found that fatherhood was associated with more conservative attitudes on all social welfare issues except spending on education and child care. We explored these anomalous results more fully in multivariate models with government spending on education and child care as the dependent variable (results not shown). We found that once age and other confounding demographic variables were controlled, fatherhood actually predicts more conservative attitudes on education spending and has no effect on day care spending. Thus, across the array of issues we examined, parenthood is associated with opposite ideological impacts for men and women.

Turning to marriage, it is interesting to note that marriage is not a significant predictor of social welfare attitudes for either women or men. Thus it is parenthood and not marriage that drives more conservative attitudes for married fathers when it comes to the role of government and government spending on social welfare policies. In alternative specifications of the model the fatherhood-marriage interaction was not significant. Additionally, the fatherhood-race interaction variable was not significant. What this indicates is that parenthood exerts a conservative influence on men across the board, regardless of the marital status or race of the father.

Parenthood, Marriage, Race and Attitudes on War and Defense

The previous chapter showed that over the past several decades mothers have sometimes been more liberal on defense and military-related issues than women without children, and that in no decades were mothers more "aggressive" or conservative in their military or defense attitudes. The more sophisticated analyses presented in this chapter further support the "maternal thinking" theory articulated by Sara Ruddick that motherhood fosters more pacifist views. Table 6.2 shows that motherhood acts as a significant predictor of more liberal or anti-war attitudes on the Iraq War index, even after variables such as partisanship, marriage, race, region, religiosity, and income are controlled. This result fairly strongly rebukes the idea that mothers were more likely to support the Iraq War and other military measures as a way of protecting their families, which was emphasized in many "Security Mom" stories. On the contrary, the results suggest that motherhood leads to less support for aggressive military actions. We believe this effect is rooted in the role of mothers as protectors and nurturers of their children. Not only are mothers concerned with sending their own

Table 6.2. Iraq War Attitudes by Parenthood with Demographic
Controls

	Women only	Men only
Parent	−.149**	−.016
	(.055)	(.071)
Married	.150**	.166*
	(.054)	(.070)
Age	.000	.000
	(.002)	(.002)
Income	.008+	−.005
	(.005)	(.006)
Education	.000	.012
	(.012)	(.013)
Religiosity	.132**	.085**
	(.022)	(.025)
Employed	−.002	−.047
	(.056)	(.073)
South	.234**	.036
	(.051)	(.058)
Minority	−.245**	.053
	(.063)	(.073)
Party ID	.263**	.321**
	(.012)	(.016)
N	977	855
R^2	.477	.385

Source: 2008 NES Data.

** p<.01, * p<.05, + p<.10, two-tailed tests.

Note: Cell entries in columns one and two are unstandardized OLS coefficients.
Standard errors are in parentheses.

children off to war but there may be something about the process
of nurturing and caring for children that leads to more pacifist
views across the board.

Although not shown, motherhood was not a predictor of more liberal attitudes in similar multivariate models with defense spending as the dependent variable. We believe a central reason why we found a significant motherhood effect on the Iraq War index, but not on the issue of defense spending, is that mothers are uniquely sensitive to national security issues that are most explicitly linked to military action and the potential loss of life, the most prominent example of which would be the Iraq War. Moreover, it is important to point out that in every year from 1980 through the present, mothers, like women overall, were significantly more liberal than fathers and men on the issue of defense spending—a finding repeated in 2008. In other words, while mothers are not uniquely liberal on defense spending compared to their non-mother counterparts, they are distinctively liberal compared to fathers and men, which is, once again, a very different reality than the image captured by the "Security Mom" label.

Interestingly, while parenthood significantly predicts more liberal attitudes on the Iraq War index for women, marriage significantly predicts more conservative attitudes. The polarizing impact of marriage and parenthood on women's views on the Iraq War is not altogether surprising since these two adult socialization experiences affect the lives of women in very different ways in terms of their day-to-day lifestyles, economic situation, and most pressing worries. These findings reinforce the need to analyze marriage and parenthood separately and not assume these two life experiences have reinforcing impacts, as some academic and popular news articles have done. Finally, it is important to note that we ran motherhood-marriage interactions as well as motherhood-race interactions in both the Iraq War and defense spending models and they were not significant. These non-significant results further underscore our argument that for women, it is simply being a mother that leads to more liberal attitudes in this policy realm, and such effects are not heightened among married or single women, white or minority women.

Being a father is not associated with distinctive views on the Iraq War index or on defense spending (not shown), but being married has a significant and conservative effect in both models for men. The results suggest that the parenting experience does not have the same impact on men as it does on women, a result consistent with the gendered parental roles of men and women. Since women are more involved in the nurturing aspect of childrearing it makes sense that they are more sensitive to the potential loss of life war represents. In comparison to women, men are more supportive of the war and of defense spending—but it is their role as husbands, not their role as fathers that helps to drive this conservatism. It is also important to note that marriage-parent interactions and parent-race interactions were not significant in any of these models.

Parents, Marriage, Race and Cultural Values Issues

We turn now to the third policy area, cultural values issues. The last chapter revealed that despite conventional wisdom that parents are a conservative bloc on family values–type issues, that there were very few motherhood effects in this issue realm. The more sophisticated analyses confirm this non-finding. Tables 6.3 and 6.4 indicate that parenthood is not a significant predictor of women's attitudes on abortion or gay marriage. Marriage, however, is a very significant predictor of more conservative attitudes for women on both of these cultural values issues. In neither case, though, is there a significant interaction between marriage and motherhood or between race and motherhood.

As discussed previously, much conventional wisdom and media commentary suggests that parents are a distinctively conservative group on values issues such as abortion and gay marriage because of their desire to protect their children from what they perceive to be negative societal influences (e.g., Barnes 1992; Brooks 2004; Greenberg 2001; Sailer 2004; Whitehead 2004). This conventional wisdom is wrong for women. Our regression results reveal that there is something about marriage—or choosing to get married—that is associated with more conservative attitudes on cultural values issues for women, but that "something" is not having and raising children.

In contrast to women, parenthood is a significant predictor of attitudes on abortion for men. Table 6.4 shows that fatherhood predicts more conservative attitudes on abortion. This finding is consistent with the results in the previous chapter revealing that abortion was characterized by some of the most consistent, conservative fatherhood effects of all the twenty-plus issues we examined.

Table 6.3. Abortion Attitudes by Parenthood with Demographic
Controls

	Women only	Men only
Parent	−.167	.446*
	(.196)	(.216)
Married	.656**	.319
	(.190)	(.205)
Age	−.009	−.002
	(.006)	(.007)
Income	−.070**	−.033+
	(.017)	(.017)
Education	−.128**	−.150**
	(.042)	(.039)
Religiosity	.591**	.477**
	(.075)	(.075)
Employed	−.024	.000
	(.187)	(.230)
South	.358*	.404*
	(.180)	(.179)
Minority	.114	.723*
	(.224)	(.222)
Party ID	.294**	.271**
	(.043)	(.050)
N	520	410
R^2	.288	.249

Source: 2008 NES Data.

** p<.01, * p<.05, + p<.10, two-tailed tests.

Note: Cell entries in columns one and two are unstandardized OLS coefficients.
Standard errors are in parentheses.

In our initial model on gay marriage, table 6.4, neither parenthood nor marriage were significant predictors for men, but when a
married-parent interaction was added to the model, not only was
it significant, but the parent variable becomes significant as well.

Table 6.4. Gay Marriage Attitudes by Parenthood with
Demographic Controls

	Women only	Men only
Parent	**.005**	**.204**
	(.141)	**(.158)**
Married	**.662****	**−.064**
	(.137)	**(.156)**
Age	.031**	.036**
	(.004)	(.005)
Income	−.040**	−.005
	(.012)	(.014)
Education	−.059*	−.135**
	(.030)	(.030)
Religiosity	.555**	.428**
	(.055)	(.057)
Employed	.384*	−.002
	(.142)	(.163)
South	.386**	.021
	(.124)	(.132)
Minority	.383*	.120
	(.157)	(.164)
Party ID	.230**	.224
	(.031)	(.036)
N	1105	926
Pseudo R²	.277	.228

Source: 2008 NES Data.

** p<.01, * p<.05, + p<.10, two-tailed tests.

Note: Cell entries in columns one and two are ordered logit coefficients. Standard errors are in parentheses.

The results suggest that not only are fathers more conservative on gay marriage but that for men the combination of marriage and parenthood heightens this conservative impact. These results are consistent with the idea that men respond to becoming parents by "defending" their life choices and families from what they perceive to be immoral or threatening cultural influences.

Parenthood, Marriage, Race and Political Orientation

In addition to examining parenthood effects in specific issue domains, we also looked at the impact of parenthood on broader political forces: ideology, partisanship, and vote choice. In the previous chapter we did not find motherhood to be significantly associated with any of these three attitudes, and these "non-results" are confirmed in this chapter. As table 6.5 indicates, motherhood was not a significant predictor of political ideology, nor was it a predictor of partisanship (results not shown), nor was it a predictor of 2008 presidential vote choice (table 6.6). Marriage is also not a predictor for ideology or vote choice for women, but is a predictor of more Republican partisanship (model not shown).

A fair amount of media coverage has implied that parents, especially married parents, are a conservative voting bloc and that Democrats must become more conservative in order to win over this group and win elections. The lack of motherhood effects on ideology, partisanship, and vote choice underscore an important point—that this conventional wisdom is wrong when it comes to women. Being a mother does not push women in a conservative direction. And while it is the case that marriage is a predictor of more Republican partisanship for women, parenthood does not contribute to this effect. Moreover, when marriage-motherhood interactions were added to the ideology, partisanship, and vote choice models, they were not significant, indicating that the combination of marriage and parenthood is not associated with a distinctively conservative politics for women.

The non-impact of motherhood on 2008 presidential vote choice is also interesting since much of the media coverage of the election focused on how Republican vice presidential nominee Sarah Palin's status as a "Hockey Mom" and mother of five

Table 6.5. Political Ideology by Parenthood with Demographic Controls

	Women only	Men only
Parent	**.115**	**.178***
	(.074)	**(.080)**
Married	**−.051**	**.204****
	(.071)	**(.078)**
Age	.007**	.003
	(.002)	(.002)
Income	.006	.002
	(.006)	(.007)
Education	−.050**	−.019
	(.015)	(.015)
Religiosity	.255**	.138**
	(.028)	(.028)
Employed	−.051	−.148
	(.074)	(.083)
South	.081	.087
	(.066)	(.066)
Minority	.043	.119
	(.083)	(.083)
Party ID	.357**	.356**
	(.016)	(.018)
N	1138	361
R^2	.390	.368

Source: 2008 NES Data.

** $p<.01$, * $p<.05$, + $p<.10$, two-tailed tests.

Note: Cell entries in columns one and two are unstandardized OLS coefficients. Standard errors are in parentheses.

Table 6.6. Republican Vote by Parenthood with Demographic Controls

	Women only	Men only
Parent	**.294**	**.141**
	(.286)	**(.332)**
Married	**.275**	**.211**
	(.268)	**(.328)**
Age	.025**	.022*
	(.009)	(.010)
Income	.017	.013
	(.026)	(.026)
Education	.046	.022
	(.061)	(.063)
Religiosity	.310**	.358**
	(.103)	(.121)
Employed	.308	.740*
	(.283)	(.362)
South	1.013**	.069
	(.253)	(.275)
Minority	−1.920**	−1.839**
	(.386)	(.370)
Party ID	1.059**	1.026**
	(.072)	(.082)
N	820	578
Pseudo R^2	.547	.534

Source: 2008 NES Data.

** $p<.01$, * $p<.05$, + $p<.10$, two-tailed tests.

Note: Cell entries in columns one and two are binary logit coefficients. Standard errors are in parentheses.

might appeal to parents, particularly mothers. The results indicate that the Republican ticket did not benefit from any motherhood bump in 2008. Additionally, further analysis revealed that Sarah Palin held no special appeal for mothers. In a regression analysis using feeling thermometer ratings toward Sarah Palin as the dependent variable, we found no significant effects for mothers or fathers (results not shown).

Table 6.5 shows that both fatherhood and marriage are significant predictors of a more conservative ideology for men. And along similar lines, while neither fatherhood nor marriage are predictors of partisanship in our initial models, when a parent-marriage interaction term is added to the partisanship model for men, both marriage and the marriage-parenthood interaction are significant. The marriage coefficient is positive showing that marriage predicts more Republican partisanship and the significant interaction effect indicates that this conservative effect is particularly the case for married fathers. Neither parenthood nor marriage predicted vote choice in the 2008 presidential election for men. Similar to analyses of the marriage gap in other years, once partisanship, income, education, and race are controlled for, the conservative effect of marriage disappears (Plutzer and McBurnett 1991; Weisberg 1987).

The Politics of Parenthood, Race, and Marriage Overview

The analyses presented in this chapter reinforce the central finding of the previous chapter that parenthood is a very important agent of adult political socialization. Being a mother and being a father has robust and statistically significant impact on a range of important policy issues, even when confounding variables are controlled. Parenthood is not only political, but it is polarizing, pushing women and men in opposite ideological directions. Our results suggest their role as nurturers of children sensitizes mothers to the need for more government social welfare programs and pushes them to develop more liberal attitudes on war-related issues. In contrast, fathers have distinctively conservative views on social welfare issues and appear to view an active social welfare state as an intrusion on their ability to provide for their families.

Additionally fathers have more conservative views on abortion and married fathers are particularly conservative on gay marriage, suggesting they are drawn to defend their traditional life choices of marriage and children in a time when such choices are becoming less common.

We were also interested in exploring how parenthood effects compare to and interact with the closely connected experience of marriage. While the number of women having children outside of the institution of marriage has increased over the past several decades, it is still the case that most parents are married. For men, parenthood and marriage act as reinforcing influences, both pushing men in a more conservative direction, and in some cases married fathers were particularly conservative. For women, though, marriage and parenthood have very different impacts. Being married either has no effect or has conservative impacts on women's political attitudes in our models. In contrast, parenthood consistently has a liberal impact for women. Thus rather than reinforcing adult socialization experiences, parenthood and marriage appear to exert cross-pressures on women. Combining marriage and parenthood into one variable as some studies have done may very well wash out the very distinct effects of these two life experiences. Moreover, our results make clear that there is something about marriage, beyond the distinctive demographics of the sub-set of women who choose to enter the institution, that exerts a politically conservative influence, but that "something," contrary to conventional wisdom, is not children.

We were also interested in understanding how parenthood interacted with race. Parents are an increasingly diverse group in terms of race and ethnicity, and minority groups tend to be more liberal on social welfare and defense issues. However, we found no evidence that the effects of being a mother or father varied by race. Only one of our eighteen parent-race interaction variables ended up being significant, and that one indicated that white women were more strongly liberalized by the effect of parenthood than non-white women. Our results strongly support the idea that being a mother fosters more liberal political attitudes and being a father fosters more conservative attitudes across the board, without regard to race or ethnicity.

7

The Consequences and Future
of the Politics of Parenthood

This book has told the story of how parenthood and the family have become politicized in contemporary American politics. The politicization of parenthood has not been a purely elite-level, nor a purely mass-level phenomenon, but has characterized all of the key components of the electoral environment: the policies of the political parties, the rhetoric of presidential candidates, the news media's election coverage, and regular Americans who are mothers and fathers. The politicization of parenthood at the mass and elite levels has been driven by and reflected fundamental shifts in American society and the structure of the American family, and in turn, has significantly shaped contemporary elections, candidates, and campaigns.

Political parties and presidential candidates turned to the language of the family and started emphasizing policies targeted directly at parents in response to the unraveling of the traditional family and as anxiety about the state and strength of the American family became more pervasive in American society. Additionally, the parties have politicized parenthood as a strategic move to secure an electoral edge in a highly competitive political environment. The news media echoed and magnified the parent and family emphasis of the parties, realizing that family frames and parent-labels such as "Security Moms" and "Hockey Moms" were an easy and attractive way to frame and sell stories about politics. Turning to the mass level, this book documents that on many important policy issues, mothers and fathers are distinctive blocs in the American electorate. In other words, parenthood is indeed political, but in different ideological directions for women and men.

We argue that the broad politicization of parenthood documented in this book has important implications for our theoretical understandings in American politics as well as practical electoral politics. More specifically, this exploration into the politicization of parenthood and the family enriches our understanding of public opinion, partisan messaging, and representation; raises concerns about political reporting; and holds potential consequences for future election outcomes. In this concluding chapter we explore these broader implications and lay out several avenues for further research on the politics of parenthood.

Parenthood and Political Socialization

What citizens believe and why they believe it are crucial questions in a democracy. This is one of the central reasons why political scientists have spent so much time studying public opinion. Scholars have produced important and informative research looking at the way several different adult life experiences including marriage, joining the workforce, and growing older impact political views. This book represents the first systematic look at the political impact of one of life's most life-changing experiences, having and raising children. Parenthood changes one's life in profound ways, socially, economically, and psychologically. This book has demonstrated that parenthood is politically significant as well. Parents hold attitudes that are significantly different than those without children in the home on a fairly broad range of important policy issues. Documenting empirically that parenthood does in fact shape public opinion adds richness to our understanding of political attitude formation and attitude change across the life cycle.

Admittedly, our results are based on cross-sectional analysis, which prevents us from controlling for selection into parenthood and proving causality. Nevertheless, we strongly suspect that the parenthood effects revealed in our analyses are not purely the product of selection effects. It seems implausible, for example, that women with distinctively liberal attitudes on social welfare issues would be so much more likely to have children than women with more conservative views. Moreover, the socialization literature provides a strong theoretical foundation for expecting that parenthood would shape the political attitudes of parents. We hope that our work on parenthood as an agent of adult political socialization is just the beginning, and that it inspires more scholarly work in this interesting and important area of social science.

One important avenue of future research will be to explore the effects of parenthood on political attitudes with a specific focus on variations in the parenting experience. For example, we would be interested in knowing whether the age of children significantly mediates parenthood effects. In other words, are mothers of young children particularly supportive of government efforts to provide day care? Are fathers of teenagers particularly conservative on cultural values issues such as abortion and gay marriage? Additionally, future research could explore whether it is simply becoming a parent that politicizes mothers and fathers, or whether the political impact of parenthood increases with the number of children in the household. We are also intrigued by existing research indicating that men in particular may react to parenthood differently depending on the sex of their children. One study found that fathers tend to be more involved in the parenting process when they have sons rather than daughters (Harris and Morgan 1991), which in turn could have political consequences. Another research project found that support for feminism and egalitarianism was higher among Canadian fathers of daughters than among men who had only sons, although the researchers found no difference among American men (Warner 1991). It would be interesting to see if the sex of children influences the particular way both mothers and fathers are politicized in contemporary U.S. politics. For example, are mothers of sons particularly anti-war? Are fathers of daughters especially conservative on issues of abortion?

Another fruitful line of research would be exploring the life-long impact of parenthood. If having and raising a child is the profound socialization experience that we argue it is in this book, it is likely that at least some of the political effects of parenthood may last for a lifetime. Moreover, for very few parents do the psychological and economic realities of being a parent completely stop when their children turn eighteen. For a sizable number of parents, grown children remain in the home after turning eighteen or return to the home after completing college, further emphasizing the need to explore the impact of parenthood over the entire life cycle.

Yet another avenue of future research would be to create nationally representative data sets that measure parenting and parental involvement in a more nuanced and sophisticated way. The measure of parenthood employed in this book, and in all social science studies on parenting, defines parenting as a dichotomous variable, indicating whether respondents are a parent of a child under eighteen in their home. While being a parent or not represents a very significant life change, we also recognize that time and energy invested in parenting varies significantly. Some parents spend every waking hour with their children, know their children's friends' names, and place their social identify as a parent before all else. For others, parenting takes up less of their time and mental energies. In a pilot study we previously conducted, we found empirical evidence that it was not just being a parent that had political consequences, but the level of involvement in the parental role (Elder and Greene 2008). The creation of a data set with more nuanced measures of parenting, or the addition of such measures to existing data sets, would allow for a deeper and more sophisticated understanding of what it is about the parenting process that fosters a different political orientation.

Another way to build on our knowledge in this area would be to collect panel data, tracking the political attitudes of women and men over time before and after they become parents. Jill Greenlee (2010) has done some interesting work along these lines looking at the effects of motherhood using panel data from the 1965 Political Socialization Study. Unfortunately this 1965 panel data is limited in what it can contribute to our understanding of the contemporary politics of parenthood. As Greenlee notes there are very few relevant issues asked across the panels and no questions tapping any social welfare issues. Thus, she is only able to track the attitudes of mothers on three issues: views on drug legalization, feelings toward the police, and feelings toward the military (Greenlee 2010, 411). Additionally, these panel data only allow for the study of women who became mothers during the civil rights movement and Vietnam War era, periods in our nation's history that were most likely not typical in terms of attitudes on these three issues. A fruitful avenue for further research, therefore, is the creation of a new longitudinal data set including detailed questions about parenthood, parental involvement, and a wide range of policy attitudes.

Parenthood and the Gender Gap

An important feature of the politics of parenthood is the way it contributes to and reinforces the gender gap. A gender gap has characterized American presidential elections since 1980 and has characterized public opinion on social welfare and use-of-force issues even longer (Andersen 1996; Kaufmann and Petrocik 1999). Although the gender gap is a much-studied topic, political scientists have not yet been able to fully explain the underlying dynamics that explain these persistent gender differences. Some earlier research on the gender gap assumed that the gendered nature of parenthood might be a force behind the gap, but the empirical research included in this book provides the first systematic and comprehensive evidence supporting the idea. Our analyses reveal that on political issues that have historically been characterized by a significant gender gap in political attitudes, most prominently social welfare policy and war-related policies, it appears that having and raising children contributes to the gap by pushing women in a liberal direction and pushing men in a conservative direction.

On a related note, our results underscore the extent to which parenting is still a highly gendered experience, even in the twenty-first century, and that the ramifications of family life and the household division of parenting responsibilities extend to the political realm. The results lend support to the maternal thinking theory advanced by some feminist scholars that the act of mothering or nurturing children fosters more compassionate and liberal attitudes on a fairly broad range of issues. In contrast, men respond to parenthood in ways consistent with societal expectations for fathers: They support more conservative "family values" types of policies and see the enlargement of the social welfare state as impinging on their ability to provide for their families economically. The polarizing impact of parenthood on women and men is then reinforced by the divergent messages about pro-family policy emerging from the two parties.

In the coming decades it will be interesting to see whether the politics of parenthood remain a polarizing force or evolve in new directions. While men and women continue to take different roles in the parenting process, time diary studies indicate that fathers have been becoming more involved as parents. They also indicate that a small but growing number of fathers are the primary care-givers of their children. Employing the more nuanced measures of parental involvement discussed previously, it would be interesting to see if fathers heavily involved in the nurturing of their children react to parenthood in a manner more similar to women. In other words, does the liberalizing effect of maternal thinking apply to all adults deeply engaged in childrearing regardless of sex? And on a broader societal level, it will be interesting to see whether the poli-tics of fatherhood become more like the politics of motherhood if indeed parental roles become less gendered and more uniform across male and female parents. Another interesting way to exam-ine this same issue would be to explore the impact of parenthood across established democracies, including countries where fathers have historically played a larger role in child care. Iversen and Rosenbluth (2006) examined how labor market opportunities for women and the gender division of labor in the household affected the gender gap across nations, and it would be interesting to incor-porate a parenthood variable into such studies.

The high-pressure balancing act of mothers, which appears to be a central force behind the liberal motherhood effect, seems unlikely to alter in a significant way in the coming decades. Given the nature of the American economy in the twenty-first century, it is unlikely mothers will retreat from the workforce. If anything, mothers may be expected to increase their hours at work. At the same time surveys reveal that mothers of the twenty-first century are absolutely committed to spending a lot of quality time with their children, and in fact, despite their increased work obligations, are managing to spend more time with their children than moth-ers of previous generations. Given the high-stress, time-crunched reality for contemporary women with children, it is likely mother-hood will continue to be a politicizing experience.

The divergent effects of parenthood on women and men are also important in reminding us that the family unit is not a cohesive political unit. The preferences of mothers and fathers are quite different, and the experience of having children can in fact drive husbands and wives, men and women, further apart. On an empirical level, the polarizing impact of parenthood by gender means that it is important to analyze parenthood results separately for women and men in future analyses. Comparing parents as a group to non-parents as some studies have done (Arnold and Weisberg 1996; Barnes 1992; Teixeira 2002) actually produces an inaccurate picture of parents on most policy issues and political variables. For example, on many of the issues examined in this study parents were a more conservative group than non-parents, but when separated by sex as presented in this book, we see that these effects were driven solely by male parents and often masked a liberal parental effect for women.

Media (Mis)Representation of the Politics of Parenthood

In addition to contributing to our theoretical understanding of political socialization and the gender gap, the results presented in this book have social and practical implications. The news media have increasingly relied on parenthood and the family as a way of making sense of campaign events, policy disputes, and the choices before voters during presidential elections. One of the problematic aspects of the politicization of parents within election news coverage has been that it has occurred without references to empirical data on the actual policy preferences of parents. And what the analyses presented in this book show is that in several important ways the news media are getting the story quite wrong in their reporting of the politics of parenthood.

First, much commentary in the news media has suggested that parents as a group have conservative leanings, and that candidates need to become more conservative to get the votes of this group (e.g., Barnes 1992; Brooks 2004; Kotkin and Frey 2004). These stereotypes about the politics of parenthood are half true at best. Fathers are more conservative than their non-father counterparts on a range of important policy issues, but all of the motherhood effects uncovered in our research were in a liberal direction. Mothers want to see a more active government when it comes to providing for families, the elderly, the poor, and other disadvantaged groups in society. Mothers also want peace, not war. Moreover, mothers are a distinctively Democratic voting bloc. While being married is associated with more conservative attitudes on some policy issues for women, our research shows that having children is not the driver behind these conservative views.

Moreover, discussing parents as a cohesive political bloc, as many news stories do, is problematic for the reasons described previously. It obscures the gendered nature and effects of parenthood in the twenty-first century. Parenthood is political, but in a distinctly different way for women and men. The news media, like social science research, needs to be careful to differentiate between the politics of motherhood—a distinctively liberal politics—and the politics of fatherhood, which is associated with more conservative views, especially on role of government and cultural values issues.

Finally, the news media have enjoyed using parent labels such as "Soccer Moms" and "Security Moms" in their election coverage. These labels often provide important frames for how society thinks about and approaches the election. As discussed previously, the "Security Mom" label that dominated much news coverage in the 2004 presidential election, and to a lesser extent the 2008 election, is clearly inaccurate. As of 2008, mothers are actually less supportive of the Iraq War than other women, even when confounding variables are controlled. Similarly, chapter 5 revealed that over the past several decades mothers have been more liberal than other women, as well as more liberal than men and fathers, on several other defense, national security, and foreign policy issues. Thus more accurate labels to describe the politics of mothers would be "Anti-War Mothers" or "Pro-Peace Mothers." Along the same lines, labels such as "Social Welfare Mothers" or "Health Care Moms" would more accurately represent the distinctive politics of mothers than the ones that have dominated news media coverage of elections.

It is troubling that the media would spend so much time discussing characterizations of parents and parental groups that are not based in reality. Political elites as well as citizens look to the news media to better understand the American political landscape and mind. And the picture the news media are presenting of the politics of parenthood is quite inaccurate. More accurate coverage of the politics of parents would frame electoral choices in a very different way. For example, Susan Carroll (2008) argued that the news media's heavy use of the term "Security Moms" in the 2004 election provided an advantage to the reelection campaign of Republican president George W. Bush. She writes, "Attention to security moms complemented the Republican campaign strategy and helped to keep the public focused on the issue where they thought Bush was strongest" (Carroll 2008, 87). Moreover, the "Security Mom" label enabled President Bush to remain focused on the theme of national security, while also appearing to respond to the concerns of women, especially mothers (Carroll 2008; Ferguson 2005).

If the news media employed accurate, empirically based parent labels such as "Pro-Peace Moms," the public might be primed to look more skeptically at campaign pledges to spend more money on war, defense, and national security. Candidates could no longer promote aggressive military policies and claim that by doing so they are responding to the concerns of mothers and their families. Moreover, media labels such as "Pro-Government Moms" might pressure candidates to articulate their plans for helping the needy and disadvantaged in a more central way in their campaigns. In other words, in order to appear responsive to the concerns of mothers, candidates might need to actually offer policies addressing their distinctive policy concerns.

The research presented in the book, therefore, offers a much-needed, accurate empirical picture of parents' political attitudes. Such knowledge could act as an important first step in dispelling and combating parenthood myths and inaccurate labels, and provide a basis for more accurate portrayals of the policy preferences of this highly salient political group.

Democrats, Republicans, and the Competition for the Votes of Parents

Starting in the 1980s, but even more in the decades since, the two major parties have been trying to top one another in appealing to the concerns of parents. According to 2008 exit polls, parents of children under eighteen formed about 40 percent of the electorate. While this is a smaller segment of the electorate than parents formed a half century ago, it is nevertheless a sizable bloc of

voters. Whichever party or candidate is more successful in appealing to parents has a definite edge toward victory in this extremely
divided electorate. Additionally, there is very little or no cost in
pushing a pro-family agenda. Family and parenting themes are
classic valence issues that have broad appeal even among those
who are not parents. Given this, we expect parenthood to remain
prominent in the appeals of both parties and in shaping political
attitudes in future elections.

While both the Republican and Democratic parties have
increasingly leaned on the language of parenthood and the family
to frame and form the basis of their policy agendas, they offer distinct visions of what pro-family policies look like. The Democratic
Party argues that family values means funding government programs from social security to education. Meanwhile, Republicans
argue that big government threatens the American family, and that
lower taxes, fewer regulations, as well as policies to support traditional values is the true pro-family agenda. Given these different
messages about the family, our empirical analyses combined with
demographic trend data suggest that the politics of parenthood
should increasingly favor the Democratic Party as the twenty-first
century progresses.

First, marriage continues to decrease as an institution in
American society. In the 1950s, married couples formed about
80 percent of all households. By 2005 this figure dipped below
50 percent, driven by rising divorce rates, delayed marriage, and
an increasing number of people choosing to remain single or
cohabitate without getting married (Roberts 2007). Census data
from 2010 reveal a continuation of these trends. Thus, Republicans
appear to have secured a significant advantage among married
voters at the same time that marriage is declining as an institution
within American society.

Along these same lines, the Republican Party's emphasis on
preserving and celebrating the "traditional family" and devaluing
of single parents, as documented in chapter 3, is increasingly in
tension with the reality of family life in the twenty-first century.
While most children are still being raised in households with married parents, this figure continues to decline, even across the first
decade of the twenty-first century (Dye 2010). Close to one-third

of households with children are headed by single parents, mostly women. Moreover, in most families both parents choose to or have to work, trends that show no sign of reversing. This large group of parents may find Republican Party platform declarations that "the well-being of children is best accomplished in the environment of the home"[1] out of touch with the reality of their lives.

Additionally, U.S. Census data show that a disproportionate and growing number of children are being born to parents who are struggling economically. One-quarter of births over the first decade of the twenty-first century have been to women in poverty (Dye 2010). Moreover, a higher proportion of parents than non-parents are recipients of one or more public assistance programs (Dye 2010). Data from the 2010 U.S. Census indicate that the last decade has been a hard one economically for families, and that an even greater percentage of families and children are now living in poverty than ten years ago. Not only has the Democratic Party traditionally received more support among low-income groups, but the Republican Party's critique of government programs and spending as anti-family may be alienating to the significant number of parents relying on government programs in order to provide for their children and their families. While the Democratic Party has become more interested in championing the cause of working- and middle-class families over poor families, its broader pro-family agenda of using the government to help families is more welcoming to the growing number of parents who are struggling economically.

Finally, groups with strong Democratic ties have been experiencing higher than average birthrates. Scholarship has already shown that the changing demographics of American society will likely favor the Democratic Party (Judis and Teixeira 2002; Judis 2008), and this is especially the case for parents. As a result of both immigration and high birthrates, the percent of parents that are of Hispanic origin is growing rapidly (Dye 2010). In the twenty-first century thus far about 20 percent of births have been to women of Hispanic origin. Moreover, the birthrate among white Americans remains lower than all other racial and ethnic groups. Given the stronger Democratic identification among racial and ethnic minorities, it appears that parents of the twenty-first century are going to be increasingly Democratic.

The Politicization of Parenthood, and
Implications for Representation

In many ways the politicization of parenthood, and the increased energy and focus the political parties, presidential candidates, and news media have placed on parents, seems like a positive development for American society. After all, increased attention to the issues facing families may lead to more policies and resources geared to help them. However, the consequences of the particular ways parenthood and the family have been politicized by the parties and the news media have not all been beneficial. In fact, we argue that the politicization of parenthood has had some negative consequences for the representation and mobilization of some groups in American society including women and some sub-sets of parents.

In the 1950s and 1960s, parenthood and the family were not dominant themes in elections and elite political rhetoric, but when party platforms and political leaders did talk about them, their central emphasis was on helping needy families and disadvantaged children. Both the Democratic Party and the Republican Party identified poor families and disadvantaged children as a worrisome issue in American society. The struggles of poor families were portrayed in a fairly positive light, and both parties agreed that disadvantaged families and children were deserving of national government attention and assistance. Across the 1950s and 1960s, Republican and Democratic platforms and presidents alike spoke of the need for the federal government to provide decent and safe housing for low-income families, to help needy families pay for the heavy costs of illness and hospitals, and to provide more robust programming for very young children.

While parties today are discussing parents and children much more than they did in the 1950s and 1960s, mention of poor families has largely disappeared from their discourse. Neither party is talking about poor families as needing protection or government intervention on their behalf. Both parties have come to target their family-friendly appeals to middle-class parents. The result is the marginalization of the serious challenges confronting poor parents. This is particularly concerning given 2010 U.S. Census results showing that more children and more families are in poverty. This same bias is apparent in news coverage of parenthood and the family. While clear definitions of "Soccer Moms" or "Security Moms" are hard to come by, the presumption is that these are middle-class mothers. A label such as "Poverty Mothers" would certainly invoke a very different image than discussion of "Soccer Moms" and might even put a different set of issues on the national political agenda.

Moreover, neither party, nor the news media, appears interested in championing the cause of families in all their forms, including the small but growing number of same-sex couples and individuals with children. Most references to parents and families by the parties and the news media refer explicitly or implicitly to married, heterosexual parents—not single parents and not gay parents. As discussed in chapter 3, the Republican Party has explicitly condemned same-sex marriage as well as adoptions by gay parents. In other words, the Republican Party explicitly excludes gay parents from their definition of the American family. The Democratic Party has not been as strident in its rhetoric about the traditional family as the Republican Party, however, Democratic platforms and presidential candidates have not supported same-sex marriage, families, or adoptions either. In other words, the specific way parenthood has been politicized marginalizes rather than brings positive attention and energy to the issues confronting gay parents, much as it does for single parents and poor parents.

Additionally, prior research has demonstrated that much of the increased attention to the family and parents by both the parties and the news media has come at the expense of explicit discussions of women's and/or feminist issues (Caroll 2008, 1999; Freeman 1997; Matto 2005; Sanbonmatsu 2004, 226). As discussed in chapter 3, the Republican Party platform dropped its support for the Equal Rights Amendment in 1980 and replaced it with language supporting motherhood. The Democratic Party as well has tried to distance itself from feminist policies by embracing parenthood. Starting in the 1990s under President Clinton, "the Democratic party has reframed its support of issues of interest to women as commitments for the family" (Sanbonmatsu 2004, 211).

In the twenty-first century, the Democratic Party has even framed its support for equal pay as a family issue, rather than a gender equality issue. Parenthood and the family have been politicized in a way that allows both parties to strongly embrace the mantle of being family friendly and pro-parent, while distancing themselves from feminist policies. The abandonment of feminist and women's issues and replacement with emphasis on motherhood and families is a cause for concern since "women's issues" are not interchangeable with the interests of mothers and families. The media's growing fascination with "Moms" only reinforces this marginalization. Mary Douglas Vavrus (2000) argues that the news media shifted from discussing women as wielders of power, as in the 1992 "Year of the Woman" label, to women as defined by their family roles as illustrated in the 1996 "Soccer Moms" label. Since 1996, the mom labels have continued from the "Waitress Moms" of 1998, to the "Hockey Moms" of 2008, while discussion of a broader range of women's issues and issues dealing with gender equality in the news media have declined (Matto 2005).

Finally, there is a strange disconnect between the issues the political and media elite use parenthood and the family to discuss and the actual concerns of American parents, especially mothers. Survey evidence shows that the top concern of mothers is work-family balance and affordable quality child care (Rankin 2002). Fathers also cite the work-family balance as their biggest challenge as parents (Rankin 2002). Yet, very little elite political communication about families addresses these issues. In the wake of the 2008 presidential election, First Lady Michelle Obama indicated that she was going to make work-life balance a priority in her public agenda, but there has been very little follow-up or broader conversation about this topic on either side of the partisan aisle. Along these same lines, the dominant "parent frames" invoked by the news media say little about these issues. Thus in many ways the parties and the news media seem to have politicized an ideal of the American family, rather than captured the realities of the family in the twenty-first-century United States. In other words, both parties want the electoral benefits of being viewed as champions of the American family without truly offering solutions to the serious economic and work-life balance issues facing parents.

Directions for Further Research on the Politics of Parenthood

As we have emphasized throughout this concluding chapter, we view the research on the politicization of parenthood presented in this book as the beginning of an exciting new avenue of research that can enrich our understanding of the role of the family in contemporary politics, as well as enrich our theoretical understandings of public opinion, framing, and elections. There are numerous ways that the research presented in this book can be and should be built upon, many of which we discussed throughout the chapter. We conclude by discussing three additional avenues for future parenthood research.

First, we look forward to future research focusing on the politics of gay parents. According to 2010 census results, about 25 percent of same-sex couples are raising children under eighteen (James 2011). Moreover, an increasing number of same-sex couples are seeking to adopt children (James 2009). Even with the recent increases, gay parents only form a very small portion of parents overall, around 2 percent. While same-sex parents are definitely included as parents in our analyses, we were unable to explore the attitudes of this subgroup specifically, both because of too few cases for meaningful analysis and because the data sets used in this book did not include questions about sexual orientation.[2] We look forward to future research projects that are able explore the attitudes of gay parents specifically and provide an accurate portrait of the politics of this subgroup of mothers and fathers. Moreover, the issue of same-sex parenting is in many crucial ways even more political than the politics of heterosexual parents. Gay parents are faced with legal prohibitions on marriage in the majority of states as well as legal prohibitions on adoptions in some states. Future research exploring the politics of gay parenthood and how it relates to the overall patterns of politicization and polarization illustrated in this book would contribute to a fuller understanding of family politics in the United States.

We are also interested in exploring in a more detailed way the effect of specific family frames on both the political priorities and attitudes of different groups within the electorate. The parties, candidates, and the news media have dramatically increased their use of language referring to parents and families. Parties claim that they will "enact pro-family tax cuts" and "help America's working families." What is especially noteworthy about this evolution in political language is how expansively parent and family frames have been used. These frames have been used not just to discuss issues directly related to parenthood, such as family leave and protecting children from predators, but to discuss issues only indirectly, and not exclusively, related to the family such as economic, social welfare, and regulatory policy. Tax cuts, for example, are advocated not only for fairness or economic growth, but also "so you can spend your hard-earned money on your family." Utilizing well-designed survey experiments would be a good way to explore under what circumstances, on what policy issues, and with which voters are parent/family frames most effective, as well as the role that partisanship plays in mediating these effects. The results from such research would not only enhance our understanding of the role that parent and family frames play in contemporary politics, but equally importantly, our understanding of framing effects.

A related and very intriguing issue, beyond the scope of this book, is how candidates invoke their own families and parental status during elections and while governing, and how the electorate evaluates this information. As parenthood has become politicized it seems that it has heightened interest in the personal lives of candidates, especially presidential candidates. Presidential candidates are under more pressure than ever to offer the country a picture of an ideal and in many ways traditional family. Interest in the family life of candidates may even be greater, and judged differently, for women than men. For example, the media provided very heavy coverage of Republican Sarah Palin's husband and five children during the 2008 presidential election. Research by Brittany L. Stalsburg (2010) represents a first step in exploring the interesting issue of how voters respond to the family life of men and women candidates. Her research, based on an experiment in which she varied the candidate's gender and parental status, finds that childless women candidates are particularly disadvantaged in terms of their perceived viability and readiness for office, especially among Republican voters, and that women with young children are perceived as less viable candidates than men candidates with young children.

In sum, we see this book not as an end, but rather the beginning of a comprehensive new exploration of the role of the family and parenthood in American political life. We ourselves, and we hope others as well, will continue to explore how the contours of parenthood shape our shared political life.

Appendixes

Appendix 1

Coding for Issues for Chapter 4

POOR: Programs/actions/spending to help poor, low-income or farm families (i.e., AFDC, TANF, welfare, Medicaid, farm subsidies)

ECONOMY: economic policy / tax cuts

CHILDREN: government programs and spending that are connected to children (child care, education, Family and Medical Leave Act, CHIP health insurance program for children, head start, college loans, making college more affordable)

SOCIAL WELFARE: government social welfare programs not directly related to children: social security, Medicare, Medicaid

REGULATION: economic regulation (environment, tobacco, HMOs, pharmaceuticals)

VALUES: references to family values or traditional families; references to the appropriate role for mothers, abortion, gay marriage, stem cells

PROTECTING KIDS: Policies geared to protect children from danger (i.e., the V-chip, violence in the media, Mark Foley / sex predators; protecting children on the internet; protecting children from school violence; illegal drugs)

MILITARY: foreign policy / national security / military spending / wars / troops

OTHER:

NO ISSUE

Appendix 2

Variable Codings for Chapter 5

GSS (Official GSS variable names in parentheses)

National Spending Variables: The following variables are based on the question: "We are faced with many problems in this country, none of which can be solved easily or inexpensively. I'm going to name some of these problems, and for each one I'd like you to tell me whether you think we're spending too much money on it, too little money, or about the right amount." Response categories are 1 too little, 2 right amount, 3 too much.

Health care (natheal)

Environment (natenvir)

Crime (natcrime)

Aid to blacks (natrace)

Drug addiction and rehabilitation (natdrug)

Education (nateduc)

Military/defense (natarms)

Foreign aid (nataid)

Welfare (natfare)

Child care (natchld)

Additional Variables

Party identification (partyid): standard Michigan measure, from 0 to 6

Ideology (libcon): standard NES measure from 1 to 7

Republican vote (pres68, pres72, pres76, pres80, pres84, pres88, pres92, pres96, pres00, pres04): 1 if voted for Republican presidential candidate, 0 if Democrat

Marijuana legalization (grass): 1 for support of legalization, 2 for opposition

Death penalty (cappun): 1 for opposition to capital punishment, 2 for support

Abortion (abdefect, abnomore, abhlth, abpoor, abrape, absingle): based upon number of cases, 0 to 6, where respondent thinks abortion should be legal, e.g., birth defect, rape, financial situation, recoded so that 0 is support in every case and 6 is opposition in every case

Homosexuality (homosex): opinion on homosexual relations from 1, always right, to 4 always wrong

NES (official variable name, from cumulative file, in parentheses)

Party identification (Vcf0101): standard NES measure, from 1 to 7

Ideology (Vcf0803): standard NES measure from 1 to 7

Republican vote (Vcf0704): 1 if voted for Republican presidential candidate, 0 if Democrat

Health care (Vcf0806): 1 government insurance plan, to 7, private insurance plan

Jobs (Vcf0809): 1, government see to jobs and good standard of living to 7, let each person get ahead on own

Aid to blacks (Vcf0830): 1, government should help blacks, to 7, blacks should help themselves

Spending/services (Vcf0839): 1, government should provide more on spending and services, to 7, government should provide less

Defense spending (Vcf0843): 1, greatly reduce defense spending, to 7, greatly increase defense spending

Environment (Vcf0842): 1, greatly increase environmental regulation, to 7, greatly reduce environmental regulation

Women's role (Vcf0834): 1, women should have equal role, to 7, women's place is in the home

Military feeling thermometer (Vcf0213): warmth toward military from 0 to 100

Gays/lesbians feeling thermometer (Vcf0232): warmth toward gays/lesbians from 0 to 100, reversed so that 100 indicates more negative feelings

Gays in the military (Vcf0877a): from 1 strongly support, to 4, strongly oppose

Abortion (Vcf0837, Vcf0838): 1, abortion should always be allowed, to 4, abortion should never be allowed

Appendix 3

Variable Codings for Chapter 6

Items in parentheses indicate variable codes in 2008 NES data

Parent (V081109): Coded 1 if children under eighteen living in household, 0 otherwise

Republican vote (V085044a): 1 for McCain, 0 for Obama

Political ideology (V083069): Seven-point scale from 1, extremely liberal, to 7, extremely conservative

Party identification (V083097, V083098a, V083098b): Seven-point scale from 0, strong Democrat to 6, strong Republican

Social welfare index (V083112, V083119, V083128, V083141x, V083142x, V083145x, V083146x, V083148x): Mean value of standardized scores for: government spending / services, government support for jobs, support for government versus private health care; federal spending on: public schools, social security, aid to poor, welfare, child care. Scale ranges from −1.37 to 2.07.

Abortion (V085092x, V085093x, V085094x, V085095x, V085096x, V085097x, V085098x): Mean of response to support for legal abortion under the following conditions: nonfatal health risk to the mother, fatal health risk, cases of incest, cases of rape, cases of birth defects, financial hardship, when "wrong" child gender. Response options range from 1, favor a great deal, to 9, oppose a great deal.

Gay marriage (V083214): 1, allow gay marriage; 2, do not allow gay marriage, but allow civil unions; 3, no legal recognition

Iraq War scale (V083033x, V083103, V085210x): Mean value of response to: support for Bush's handling of war in Iraq, government's handling of war in Iraq, and whether war in Iraq has been "worth it." Ranges from 0, strongly oppose, to 3, strongly support

Defense spending (V083112): Support for government defense spending: 1, greatly decrease defense spending to 7, greatly increase

Age (V081104): Age in years

Income (V083248, V083249): Household income across twenty-five categories

Education (V083217): Years of education

Religiosity (V083181, V083182): Importance of religion to one's life, from 1, not at all, to 4, a great deal

Marital status (V083216x): 1, currently married; 0 otherwise

Employment status (V083222): 1, currently employed; 0 otherwise

Southerner (V081204): 1, resides in NES Southern region; 0 otherwise

Minority race (V083251a): 1, for non-white respondent; 0 for white respondents

Notes

Chapter 2. The Politics of the Changing American Family

1. In 2005 there were several high-profile news stories speculating that highly educated mothers were opting out of the workforce. Further research, however, showed that the 2 percentage point drop in employment among this group was parallel to other groups in society and a product of the 2001–2004 recession. Moreover, highly educated mothers remain the least likely to become stay-at-home moms (Coontz 2006).

2. The government assistance programs considered in this study were Temporary Assistance for Needy Families (TANF), Food Stamps, Special Supplemental Nutrition Program for Women, Infants, and Children (WIC), Housing Assistance, and General Assistance and other state and county-level welfare programs.

Chapter 3. "Family Values" vs. "Champion of Working Families": Parenthood, Families, and the Political Parties

1. Newly inaugurated presidents do not give a State of the Union address until their second year in office. The four most recent presidents, George Bush, Bill Clinton, George W. Bush, and Barack Obama, addressed a joint session of Congress shortly after their inaugurations. Even though these are not technically State of the Union addresses, we code them as such since their timing, length, delivery style, and media coverage are essentially the same.

2. Though not shown, the effect of time was also significant when using the party platform measure standardized for number of words.

3. Although the results are not shown, we broke down all our analyses of parent-family terms by specific term. Across the 1950s and 1960s there was a combined total of ten references to parent/parents in all the types of documents analyzed: eight in platforms, one in convention

143

speeches, none in inaugural addresses, and one in State of the Union addresses.

4. For example, the 1988 platform stated that "The God-given rights of the family come before those of government" and that "Family's most important function is to raise the next generation of Americans, handing on to them the Judeo-Christian values of western civilization and our ideals of liberty."

5. Quotes are from the 2004 Republican platform and 1992 State of the Union address.

6. 1996 State of the Union address.

7. 1980 and 1984 Democratic platforms.

8. Likewise, the classic Iyengar and Kinder (1987) experiments strongly support this view.

Chapter 4. The Rise of Politicized Moms and Dads: Media Coverage of Parenthood

1. In prior research (Elder and Greene 2006) we searched the *New York Times* and the *Washington Post* for the full calendar year of each of the five presidential elections across the 1984–2000 time period and identified the number of stories in which the keywords "children" or "family" were found in the lead paragraph of stories along with "Republican" or "Democrat." This more inclusive approach revealed the same dramatic increase albeit with much higher numbers: In 1984, there were a total of 387 parent-family themed political articles in these two newspapers, and by 2000 that number increased to 914. In this research, we also conducted parallel searches for keywords including "social security" and "military spending" for control purposes, and they did not reveal an increasing pattern. Given the similar increasing pattern across multiple news sources and with alternative search methods, we are confident the trends we identify are accurate and that the 300-plus articles from the *New York Times* on which our more detailed content analyses are based adequately reflect the overall political tenor of the mainstream media.

Chapter 5. The Political Attitudes of Mothers and Fathers

1. Prior research (Elder and Greene 2008) suggests that coding all respondents who have children in the home as parents leads to about a 10 percent false positive rate. The error rate is most likely lower with GSS data as it contains a question as to whether the respondent has ever had children, allowing us to eliminate from the parent category those respondents who are living with a child under eighteen but have never

been parents (i.e., older siblings). Even then, some respondents could be living with other people's children, for example, a grandmother living with her grandchildren.

Chapter 6. Marriage, Race, and the Politics of Parenthood

1. Kingston and Finkel (1987) and Plutzer and McBurnett (1991) show that if marriage is coded as married, single, and previously married, as opposed to just married/not married, marriage remains a significant predictor in 1984 as well.

2. In 2004, 19 percent of women forty to forty-four were childless, about twice the percentage childless among women of the same age in 1976 (Dye 2005).

3. According to 2005 Census data, only 31 percent of African Americans are married compared to 46 percent of Hispanics and 56 percent of whites (Dye 2005).

4. In 2004, 62 percent of births to black women were non-marital as compared to 32 percent for Hispanic women and 25 percent for whites (Dye 2005, 5).

5. 2001 Census data show that among black mothers with infants 56 percent were participants in a government assistance program as compared to 43 percent of Hispanic mothers and 21 percent of white mothers.

6. On Father's Day in 2008 Barack Obama gave a widely covered speech urging fathers, especially black fathers, to take more responsibility for their children. The theme of responsible fatherhood was also a part of Barack Obama's 2008 Democratic Nomination acceptance speech. The actual phrase "Responsible Fatherhood," however, comes from an initiative launched by the Obama administration in June 2009, which President Obama described as a "national conversation on responsible fatherhood and healthy families" (Cooper 2009, A10).

7. In 2008, NES began a new series of measures and questions on these long-standing issues which are not compatible with the earlier measures. Half the sample received the old questions and half the new. Unfortunately, the "new" measures largely fail to measure the core underlying concept, for example, the health care item measures only attitudes toward the new Medicare prescription drug benefit, rather than government-supported health care more broadly. Therefore, to have more reliable measures and to maintain consistency with earlier research, we constructed our scale only for the half-sample which received the traditional questions.

8. Whereas in the past NES questions on government spending had very limited response categories, the new measures are actually eight-point scales running from increased a great deal to cut out entirely.

9. As the NES contained a substantial minority over-sample, all analyses were conducted while weighting the data set according to the pre-election weight variable (v080101).

10. Following the path of Burns, Schlozman, and Verba (2001), we assess the impact of children on men and women in separate regression equations rather than simply looking at the impact of parenthood overall. We believe this is the best approach for answering our particular research questions because of our expectation that becoming parents and raising children may impact women and men differently. Using separate equations allows us to examine whether being a parent influences the attitudes of moms and dads in different directions, information that would be obscured by using one model with an interaction term for gender.

Chapter 7. The Consequences and Future of the Politics of Parenthood

1. This quote is from the 1992 Republican Party platform.

2. NES does not include a question about sexual orientation, whereas GSS added a question identifying the sexual orientation of the respondent starting in 2008.

Bibliography

Adams, Greg. 1997. "Abortion: Evidence of an Issue Evolution." *American Journalism of Political Science* 41(3): 718–738.

Andersen, Kristi. 1996. "Gender and Public Opinion." In *Understanding Public Opinion*, ed. Barbara Norrander and Clyde Wilcox. Washington, DC: CQ Press, 19–36.

Andersen, Kristi, and Elizabeth A. Cook. 1985. "Women, Work and Political Attitudes." *American Journal of Political Science*. 29: 606–625.

Anderson, Tamara, and Beth Vail. 1999. "Child-Care Dilemmas in Contemporary Families." In *American Families: A Multicultural Reader*, ed. Stephanie Coontz, Maya Parson, and Gabrielle Raley. New York: Routledge, 359–370.

Arnold, Laura, and Herbert Weisberg. 1996. "Parenthood, Family Values, and the 1992 Presidential Election." *American Politics Quarterly* 24(2): 194–220.

Bendyna, Mary E., Tamara Finucane, Lynn Kirby, John P. O'Donnell, Clyde Wilcox. 1996. "Gender Differences in Public Attitudes Toward the Gulf War: A Test of Competing Hypotheses." *The Social Science Journal* 33(1): 1–22.

Bianchi, Suzanne. 2000. "Maternal Employment and Time with Children: Dramatic Change or Surprising Continuity?" *Demography* 37(4): 401–414.

Bianchi, Suzanne M., John P. Robinson, and Melissa A. Milkie. 2006. *Changing Rhythms of American Family Life.* New York: Russell Sage Foundation.

Box-Steffensmeier, Janet M., Suzanna De Boef, and Tse-Min Lin. 2004. "The Dynamics of the Partisan Gender Gap." *American Political Science Review* 98(3): 515–528.

Budig, Michelle J., and Paula England. 2001. "The Wage Penalty for Motherhood." *American Sociological Review* 66: 204–255.

147

Burns, Nancy, Kay Lehman Schlozman, and Sidney Verba. 2001. *The Private Roots of Public Action: Gender, Equality, and Political Participation*. Cambridge, MA: Harvard University Press.

Burns, Nancy, Kay Lehman Schlozman, and Sidney Verba. 1997. "The Public Consequences of Private Inequality: Family Life and Citizen Participation." *The American Political Science Review* 91(2): 373–389.

Carmines, Edwards G., and James A. Stimson. 1989. *Issue Evolution: Race and the Transformation of American Politics*. New Jersey: Princeton University Press.

Carroll, Susan J. 2008. "Security Moms and Presidential Politics: Women Voters in the 2004 Election." In *Voting the Gender Gap*, ed. Lois Duke Whitaker. Urbana: University of Illinois Press, 75–90.

Carroll, Susan J. 1999. "The Disempowerment of the Gender Gap: Soccer Moms and the 1996 Election." *PS: Political Science and Politics* 32: 7–12.

Carroll, Susan. 1988. "Women's Autonomy and the Gender Gap: 1980 and 1982." In *The Politics of the Gender Gap: The Social Construction of Political Influence*, ed. Carol M. Mueller. Newbury Park, CA: Sage, 236–257.

Christiansen, Shawn L., and Rob Palkovitz. 2001. "Why the 'Good Provider' Role Still Matters: Providing as a Form of Paternal Involvement." *Journal of Family Issues* 22(1): 84–106.

Cohen, Jeffrey E. 1997. *Presidential Responsiveness and Public Policy Making*. Ann Arbor: University of Michigan Press.

Cohen, Jeffrey E. 1995. "Presidential Rhetoric and the Public Agenda." *American Journal of Political Science* 39(1): 87–107.

Collins, Patricia Hill. 1994. "Shifting the Center: Race, Class, and Feminist Theorizing about Motherhood." In *Representations of Motherhood*, ed. Donna Bassin, Margaret Honey, and Meryle Mahrer Kaplan. New Haven: Yale University Press, 56–74.

Conover, Pamela Johnston, and Virginia Sapiro. 1993. "Gender, Feminist Consciousness, and War." *American Journal of Political Science* 37(4): 1079–1099.

Coontz, Stephanie. 2005. *Marriage, a History: From Obedience to Intimacy, or How Love Conquered Marriage*. New York: Viking Adult.

Coontz, Stephanie. 1992. *The Way We Never Were: American Families and the Nostalgia Trap*. New York: Basic Books.

Cooper, Helene. 2009. "President Delivers Exhortation to Fathers." *New York Times*. June 20. http://www.nytimes.com/2009/06/20/us/politics/20obama.html.

Deitch, Cynthia. 1988. "Sex Differences in Support for Government Spending." In *The Politics of the Gender Gap*, ed. Carol M. Mueller. Newbury Park, CA: Sage Publications, 192–216.

Douglas, Susan J., and Meredith W. Michaels. 2004. *The Mommy Myth: The Idealization of Motherhood and How It Has Undermined All Women.* New York: Free Press.

Druckman, James N. 2004. "Political Preference Formation: Competition, Deliberation, and the (Ir)relevance of Framing Effects." *American Political Science Review* 98(4): 671–686.

Dye, Jane Lawler. 2010. *Fertility of American Women: 2008.* Current Population Reports P20-563: U.S. Census Bureau, Washington, DC.

Dye, Jane Lawler. 2005. *Fertility of American Women: June 2004.* Current Population Reports P20-555: U.S. Census Bureau, Washington, DC.

Elder, Laurel, and Steven Greene. 2008. "Parenthood and the Gender Gap." In *The Gender Gap: Voting and the Sexes.* Ed. Lois Duke Whitaker. Urbana: University of Illinois Press, 119–140.

Elder, Laurel, and Steven Greene. 2007. "The Myth of 'Security Moms' and 'NASCAR Dads: Parenthood, Political Stereotypes, and the 2004 Election." *Social Science Quarterly* 88(1): 1–19.

Elder, Laurel, and Steven Greene. 2006. "The Children Gap on Social Welfare and the Politicization of American Parents, 1984–2000." *Politics & Gender* 2(4): 451–472.

Elshtain, Jean Bethke. 1987. *Women and War.* New York: Basic.

Elshtain, Jean. 1985. "Reflections on War and Political Discourse: Realism, Just War, and Feminism in a Nuclear Age." *Political Theory* 13(1): 39–57.

Elshtain, Jean. 1983. "On Beautiful Souls, Just Warriors and Feminist Consciousness." In *Women and Men's Wars*, ed. Judith Stiehm. Oxford: Pergamon Press, 342–349.

Elshtain, Jean Bethke. 1981. *Public Man, Private Woman.* Princeton: Princeton University Press.

Ferguson, Michaele L. 2005. "'W' Stands for Women: Feminism and Security Rhetoric in the Post-9/11 Bush Administration." *Politics & Gender* 1(1): 9–38.

Fields, Jason. 2004. *America's Families and Living Arrangements: 2003.* Current Population Reports, P20-553. U.S. Census Bureau: Washington, DC.

Freeman, Jo. 1993. "Feminism vs. Family Values: Women at the 1992 Democratic and Republican Conventions." *PS: Political Science and Politics* 26(2): 21–28.

Freeman, Jo. 1997. "Change and Continuity for Women at the Republican and Democratic National Conventions." *The American Review of Politics* 18 (Winter): 353–367.

Galinsky, Ellen, Kerstin Aumann, and James T. Bond. 2008. *Times Are Changing: Gender and Generation at Work and at Home.* Families

and Work Institute. http://www.familiesandwork.org/site/research/
reports/Times_Are_Changing.pdf

Gallagher, Sally K., and Naomi Gerstel. 2001. "Connections and Constraints: The Effects of Children on Caregiving." *Journal of Marriage
and the Family* 63: 265–275.

Gerson, Kathleen. 1987. "Empowering Social Divisions among Women:
Implications for Welfare State Politics." *Politics and Society* 15:
213–21.

Gerson, Kathleen. 1985. *Hard Choices: How Women Decide about Work,
Career, and Motherhood.* Berkeley: University of California Press.

Gilens, Martin. 2000. Why Americans Hate Welfare: Race, Media, and the
Politics of Anti-Poverty Policy. Chicago: University of Chicago Press.

Graber, Doris. 2006. *Mass Media and American Politics,* 7th edition.
Washington, DC: CQ Press.

Greenberg, Anna. 2001. "The Marriage Gap." *Blueprint Magazine,* Democratic Leadership Committee. July 12, 2001.

Greenberg, Anna, and Jennifer Berktold. 2005. "Unmarried Women in the
2004 Presidential Election." Greenberg Quinlan Rosner Research,
January 2005, available at http://www.greenbergresearch.com/
index.php?ID=1225.

Greenlee, Jill. 2010. "Soccer Moms, Hockey Moms and the Question of
'Transformative' Motherhood." *Politics & Gender* 6(3): 405–432.

Greenlee, Jill. 2007. *The Political Dynamics of Parenthood.* Doctoral
dissertation, University of California Berkeley, 2007. *Dissertation
Abstracts International.*

Harris, Kathleen Mullan, and S. Philip Morgan. 1991. "Fathers, Sons, and
Daughters: Differential Paternal Involvement in Parenting." *Journal
of Marriage and the Family* 53(3): 531–544.

Hays, Sharin. 1996. *The Cultural Contradictions of Motherhood.* New
Haven, CT: Yale University Press.

Hill, Shirley A. 2001. "Class, Race, and Gender Dimensions of Child Rear-
ing in African American Families." *Journal of Black Studies* 31(4):
494–508.

Hirshman, Linda R. 2006. *Get to Work: A Manifesto for Women of the
World.* New York: Viking Adult.

Howell, Susan E., and Christine L. Day. 2000. "Complexities of the Gender Gap." *The Journal of Politics* 62: 858–874.

Iversen, Torbin, and Frances Rosenbluth. 2006. "The Political Economy of
Gender: Explaining Cross-national Variation in the Gender Division
of Labor and the Gender Voting Gap." *American Journal of Political
Science* 50(1):1–19.

Iyengar, Shanto. 1991. *Is Anyone Responsible? How Television Frames Political Issues.* Chicago: University of Chicago Press.

Iyengar, Shanto. 1987. "Television News and Citizens' Explanations of National Affairs." *American Political Science Review* 81(3): 815–831.

Iyengar, Shanto, and Donald Kinder. 1987. *News That Matters.* Chicago: University of Chicago Press.

Jacobs, Jerry A., and Kathleen Gerson. 2004. *The Time Divide: Work, Family and Gender Inequality.* Cambridge, MA: Harvard University Press.

Jacoby, William. 2000. "Issue Framing and Public Opinion on Government Spending." *American Journal of Political Science* 44(4): 450–767.

Jamieson, Kathleen Hall. 2000. *Everything You Think You Know about Politics . . . And Why You're Wrong.* New York: Basic Books.

Jamieson, Kathleen Hall, Erika Falk, and Susan Sherr. 1999. "The Enthymeme Gap in the 1996 Presidential Campaign." *PS, Political Science and Politics* 32(March): 12–16.

Jamieson, Kathleen Hall, and Paul Waldman. 2003. *The Press Effect: Politicians, Journalists, and the Stories That Shape the Political World.* Oxford: Oxford University Press.

Jennings, M. Kent. 1979. "Another Look at the Life Cycle and Political Participation." *American Journal of Political Science* 23: 755–771.

Jennings, M. Kent, and Laura Stoker. 2000. "Political Similarity and Influence between Husbands and Wives." Paper presented at the Annual Meeting of the American Political Science Association, Washington, D.C., August 30–September 2, 2000.

Judis, John B. 2008. "America the Liberal." *The New Republic.* November 19, 2008. 20–22.

Judis, John B., and Ruy Teixeira. 2002. *The Emerging Democratic Majority.* New York: Scribner.

Kaufmann, Karen, and John Petrocik. 1999. "The Changing Politics of American Men: Understanding the Source of the Gender Gap." *American Journal of Political Science* 43(3): 864–887.

Kerbel, Matthew R., Sumaiya Apee, and Marc Howard Ross. 2000. "PBS Ain't So Different: Public Broadcasting, Election Frames, and Democratic Empowerment." *The Harvard International Journal of Press/ Politics* 5(4): 8–32.

Kingston, Paul William, and Steven E. Finkel. 1987. "Is There a Marriage Gap in Politics?" *Journal of Marriage and the Family* 49: 57–64.

Kotkin, Joel, and William Frey. December 2, 2004. "Parent Trap." *The New Republic Online.* www.tnr.com/doc.mhtml?pt=sKzRTBxZkbnZ3Ru M0cWdfh%3D%3D.

Krosnick, Jon A., and Donald R. Kinder. 1990. "Altering Popular Support for the President through Priming." *American Political Science Review* 84: 497–512.

Lawless, Jennifer, and Richard Fox. 2005. *It Takes a Candidate: Why Women Don't Run for Office.* New York, NY: Cambridge University Press.

Lichter, S. Robert. 2001. "A Plague on Both Parties: Substance and Fairness in TV Election News." *The Harvard International Journal of Press/Politics* 6(3): 8–30.

Lugaila, Terry A. 2005. *Participation in Government Assistance Programs: 2001.* Current Population Reports, P70-102. U.S. Census Bureau, Washington, DC.

Luker, Kristin. 1984. *Abortion and the Politics of Motherhood.* Berkeley: University of California Press.

Lundberg, Shelly, and Elaina Rose. 2002. "The Effects of Sons and Daughters on Men's Labor Supply and Wages." *Review of Economics and Statistics* 84(2): 251–268.

Lundberg, Shelly, and Elaina Rose. 2000. "Parenthood and the Earnings of Married Men and Women." *Labour Economics* 7(6): 689–710.

Manza, Jeff, and Clem Brooks. 1998. "The Gender Gap in U.S. Presidential Elections: Why? Why? Implications?" *American Journal of Sociology* 103(5): 1235–1266.

Matto, Elizabeth. 2005. "The Politicization of Motherhood: The Increase in Attention Paid to Mothers in Campaigns and the Effect on Interests of Women in General." Paper presented at the 2005 Annual Meeting of the Northeastern Political Science Association. Philadelphia, PA.

McGlen, Nancy E. 1980. "The Impact of Parenthood on Political Participation." *The Western Political Quarterly* 33(3): 297–313.

McLanahan, Sara, and Julia Adams. 1987. "Parenthood and Psychological Well-Being." *Annual Review of Sociology* 13: 237–57.

McClain, Paula D., and Joseph Stewart Jr. 2006. *"Can We All Get Along?": Racial and Ethnic Minorities in American Politics,* 4th edition. Boulder: Westview Press.

Mendelsohn, Matthew. 1996. "The Media and Interpersonal Communications: The Priming of Issues, Leaders, and Party Identification." *Journal of Politics* 58:112–125.

Monroe, Alan D. 1983. "American Party Platforms and Public Opinion." *American Journal of Political Science* 27(1): 27–42.

Morgan, S. Philip, and Linda J. Waite. 1987. "Parenthood and the Attitudes of Young Adults." *American Sociological Review* 52: 541–547.

Munch, Allison, J. Miller McPherson, and Lynn Smith-Lovin. "Gender, Children, and Social Contacts: The Effects of Childrearing for Men and Women." *American Sociological Review* 62: 674–689.

National Annenberg Election Survey. 2004. "Despite Limited Convention Coverage Public Learned about Campaign from Democrats." Annenberg Public Policy Center, August 29, 2004. http://www.annenbergpublicpolicycenter.org/Downloads/Political_Communication/naes/2004_03_dnc-knowledge_08-30_pr.pdf.

Nelson, Thomas, and Zoe Oxley. 1999. "Issue Framing Effects on Belief Importance and Framing." *The Journal of Politics* 61(4): 1040–1067.

Nelson, Thomas, Zoe Oxley, and Rosalee Clawson. 1997. "Toward a Psychology of Framing Effects." *Political Behavior* 19: 221–246.

Nock, Stephen. 1998. *Marriage in Men's Lives.* New York: Oxford University Press.

Nomaguchi, Kei M., and Melissa A. Milkie. 2003. "Costs and Rewards of Children: The Effects of Becoming a Parent on Adults' Lives." *Journal of Marriage and Family* 65(2): 356–374.

Patterson, Thomas E. 2000. "Doing Well and Doing Good: How Soft News and Critical Journalism Are Shrinking the News Audience and Weakening Democracy—and What News Outlets Can Do About It." *The Joan Shorenstein Center. Press/Politics.*

Patterson, Thomas E. 1993. *Out of Order.* New York: Vintage Books.

Pedersen, Johannes T. 1976. "Age and Change in Public Opinion: The Case of California, 1960–1970." *Public Opinion Quarterly* 40(2): 143–153.

Petrocik, John R. 1996. "Issue Ownership in Presidential Elections, with a 1980 Case Study." *American Journal of Political Science* 40: 825–850.

Petrocik, John R., William L. Benoit, Glenn J. Hansen. 2003. "Issue Ownership and Presidential Campaigning, 1952–2000." *Political Science Quarterly* 118: 599–626.

Pew Research Center. 2010. "The Decline of Marriage and Rise of New Families." http://pewsocialtrends.org.

Pew Research Center. 2007. "As Marriage and Parenthood Drift Apart, Public Is Concerned about Social Impact." http://pewresearch.org/assets/social/pdf/Marriage.pdf.

Piven, Frances F. 1985. "Women and the State: Ideology, Power and the Welfare State." In *Gender and the Life Course,* ed. Alice S. Rossi. Hawthorne, NY: Aldine, 265–287.

Plissner, Martin. 1983. "The Marriage Gap." *Public Opinion* (February-March): 53.

Plutzer, Eric. 1988. "Work Life, Family Life, and Women's Support of Feminism." *American Sociological Review* 53(4): 640–649.

Plutzer, Eric, and Michael McBurnett. 1991. "Family Life and American Politics: The 'Marriage Gap' Reconsidered." *Public Opinion Quarterly* 55: 113–127.

Pomper, Gerald. 1980. *Elections in America.* New York: Longman.

Ponza, Michael, Greg. J. Duncan, Mary Corcoran, and Fred Groskind. 1989. "The Guns of Autumn? Age Differences in Support for Transfers to the Young and Old." *Public Opinion Quarterly* 52(4): 441–466.

Popenoe, David. 2005. *War over the Family*. New Brunswick, NJ: Transaction Press.

Popenoe, David. 1996. *Life without Father: Compelling New Evidence That Fatherhood and Marriage Are Indispensable for the Good of Children and Society*. New York: The Free Press.

Popenoe, David. 1988. *Disturbing the Nest: Family Change and Decline in Modern Societies*. New York: Aldine de Gruyter.

Rankin, Nancy. 2002. "The Parent Vote." In *Taking Parenting Public: The Case for a New Social Movement*, ed. Sylvia Ann Hewlett, Nancy Rankin, and Cornel West. Lanham, MD: Rowman and Littlefield, 251–264.

Ribuffo, Leo P. 2006. "Family Policy Past as Prologue: Jimmy Carter, the White House Conferences on Families, and the Mobilization of the New Christian Right." *Review of Policy Research* 23(2): 311–337.

Rindfuss, Ronald R., Karen L. Brewster, and Andrew L. Kavee. 1996. "Women, Work and Children: Behavioral and Attitudinal Change in the United States." *Population and Development Review* 22(3): 457–482.

Risman, Barbara J. 1998. *Gender Vertigo: American Families in Transition*. New Haven: Yale University Press.

Robinson, John P., and Geoffrey Godbey. 1999. *Time for Life: The Surprising Ways Americans Use Their Time*, 2nd edition. University Park: Pennsylvania State University Press.

Ruddick, Sara. 1989. *Maternal Thinking: Towards a Politics of Peace*. Boston: Beacon Press.

Ruddick, Sara. 1983. "Preservation Love and Military Destruction: Some Reflections on Mother and Peace." In *Mothering: Essays in Feminist Theory*, ed. Joyce Trebilcot. Totowa, NJ: Rowman and Allanheld, 231–262.

Ruddick, Sara. 1980. "Maternal Thinking." *Feminist Studies* 6: 342–347.

Sanbonmatsu, Kira. 2004. *Democrats/Republicans and the Politics of Women's Place*. Ann Arbor: University of Michigan Press.

Sapiro, Virginia. 1983. *The Political Integration of Women: Roles, Socialization, and Politics*. Urbana, IL: University of Illinois Press.

Sapiro, Virginia. 1982. "Private Costs of Public Commitments or Public Costs of Private Commitments? Family Roles and Political Ambition." *American Journal of Political Science* 25: 265–279.

Schaffner, Brian F. 2005. "Priming Gender: Campaigning on Women's Issues in U.S. Senate Elections." *American Journal of Political Science* 49(4): 803–817.

Schlozman, Kay Lehman, Nancy Burns, Sidney Verba, and Jesse Dona-
hue. 1995. "Gender and Citizen Participation: Is There a Different
Voice?" *American Journal of Political Science* 39(2): 267–293.

Schor, Juliet B. 2002. "Time Crunch among American Parents." In *Taking
Parenting Public: The Case for a New Social Movement*, ed. Sylvia
Ann Hewlett, Nancy Rankin, and Cornel West. Lanham, MD: Row-
man and Littlefield, 83–102.

Skolnick, Arlene. 1991. *Embattled Paradise: The American Family in the
Age of Uncertainty*. New York: Basic.

Stalsburg, Brittany L. 2010. "Voting for Mom: The Political Consequences
of Being a Parent for Male and Female Candidates." *Politics & Gender* 6(3): 373–404.

Stoker, Laura, and M. Kent Jennings. 2005. "Political Similarity and Influ-
ence between Husbands and Wives." In *The Social Logic of Politics:
Personal Networks as Contexts for Political Behavior*, ed. Alan S.
Zuckerman. Philadelphia: Temple University Press.

Sudarkasa, Niara. 1999. "Interpreting the African Heritage in Afro-Amer-
ican Family Organization." In *American Families: A Multicultural
Reader*, ed. Stephanie Coontz, Maya Parson, and Gabrielle Raley.
New York: Routledge, 59–73.

Tate, Katherine. 1993. *From Protest to Politics: The New Black Voters in
American Elections*. Cambridge, MA: Harvard University Press and
Russell Sage Foundation.

Teachman, Jay D., Lucky M. Tedrow, and Kyle D. Crowder. 2000. "The
Changing Demography of America's Families." *Journal of Marriage
and the Family* 64(4): 1234–1246.

Teghtsoonian, Katherine. "The Work of Caring for Children: Contradic-
tory Themes in American Child Care Policy Debates." *Women &
Politics* 17(2): 77–99.

Teixeira, Ruy. 2002. "Political Trends among American Parents: The 1950s
to 1996." In *Taking Parenthood Public*, Sylvia Ann Hewlett, Nancy
Rankin, and Cornel West. Lanham, MD: Rowman and Littlefield,
119–138.

Terkildsen, Nayda, and Frauke Schnell. 1997. "How Media Frames Move
Public Opinion: An Analysis of the Women's Movement." *Political
Research Quarterly* 50(4): 879–900.

Thornton, Arland, and Linda Young-DeMarco. 2001. "Four Decades of
Trends in Attitudes toward Family Issues in the United States:
The 1960s through the 1990s." *Journal of Marriage and Family* 63:
1009–1037.

Tinnick, Jim. 2003. "The Marriage Gap: Fact or Fiction." *Perspectives: Elec-
tronic Journal of the American Association of Behavioral and Social
Sciences*. Volume 6. http://aabss.org.journal2003/.

Townsend, Nicholas. 2002. *The Package Deal: Marriage, Work, and Fatherhood in Men's Lives*. Philadelphia: Temple University Press.

Vavrus, Mary Douglas. 2000. "From Women of the Year to 'Soccer Moms': The Case of the Incredible Shrinking Women." *Political Communication* 17: 193–213.

Waite, Linda J., and Maggie Gallagher. 2000. *The Case for Marriage: Why Married People Are Happier, Healthier, and Better Off Financially*. New York: Doubleday.

Walters, Ronald. 1990. "Party Platforms as Political Process." *PS: Political Science and Politics*. 3(3): 436–438.

Warner, Rebecca L. 1991. "Does the Sex of Your Children Matter? Support for Feminism among Women and Men in the United States and Canada." *Journal of Marriage and the Family*. 53(4): 1051–1056.

Wattenberg, Martin P. 2004. "The Changing Presidential Media Environment." *Presidential Studies Quarterly* 34(3): 557–572.

Wattenberg, Martin P. 1998. *The Decline of American Political Parties, 1952–1996*. Cambridge, MA: Harvard University Press.

Weisberg, Herbert F. 1987. "The Demographics of a New Voting Gap: Marital Differences in American Voting." *Public Opinion Quarterly* 55: 335–343.

Welch, Susan, and John Hibbing. 1992. "Financial Conditions, Gender and Voting in American National Elections." *The Journal of Politics* 54: 197–213.

West, Laurel Parker. 2004. "Welfare Queens, Soccer Moms and the Working Poor: The Socio-Political Construction of State Child Care Policy." PhD dissertation Emory University.

Whitehead, Barbara Dafoe. December 17, 2004. "The Marriage Gap: When Will the Democrats Wake Up?" *Commonweal* 131 (22): 10–11.

Wisensale, Steven K. 1997. "The White House and Congress on Child Care and Family Leave Policy: From Carter to Clinton." *Policy Studies Journal* 25(1):75–86.

Wisensale, Steven K. 1992. "Toward the 21st Century: Family Change and Public Policy." *Family Relations* 41(4): 417–422.

Wolbrecht, Christina. 2000. *The Politics of Women's Rights*. Princeton, NJ: Princeton University Press.

Wolff, Edward N. 2002. "The Economic Status of Parents in Postwar America." In *Taking Parenting Public: The Case for a New Social Movement*, ed. Sylvia Ann Hewlett, Nancy Rankin, and Cornel West. Lanham, MD: Rowman and Littlefield. 59–82.

Zaller, John R., and Stanley Feldman. 1992. "A Simple Theory of the Survey Response: Answering Questions Versus Revealing Preferences." *American Journal of Political Science* 36(3): 579–616.

Newspaper Articles

Alberts, Sheldon. "Candidates Address 'Security Moms." *The Gazette (Montreal)*. 19 October, 2004. A22.

Allen, Mike. "Bush Makes Pitch to 'Security Moms." *Washington Post*. 18 September, 2004. A14.

Allen, Mike, and Lois Romano. "Presidential Candidates Aim Messages at Women." *The Washington Post*. 23 October, 2004. A6

Associated Press. "From NASCAR Dad to Soccer Mom, Campaigns Drawn to Political Labels." *The Post-Standard*. 11 June, 2004.

Barnes, Fred. "The Family Gap." *Reader's Digest*, July 1992. 48–54.

Baskerville, Stephen. "NASCAR Dads, Soccer Moms, and Latchkey Kids." *Human Events Online*, www.humaneventsonline.com/article. php?print=yes&id=3190 (Accessed July 14, 2004).

Belkin, Lisa. "When Mom and Dad Share It All." *New York Times*. June 15, 2008. http://www.nytimes.com/2008/06/15/magazine/15parenting-t.html?pagewanted=print.

Birnbaum, Jeffrey H., and Chris Cillizza. " 'Mortgage Moms' May Star in Midterm Vote." *Washington Post*. 5 September, 2006. A1.

Blyth, Myrna. "Determined Housewives." *National Review*. 10 November, 2004.

Brooks, David. "The New Red-Diaper Babies." *New York Times*. 7 December, 2004.

Calabresi, Massimo. "Battling for the Show-Me Moms." *Time*. 29 October, 2006.

Clarke, Liz. "In Sun Belt, Politicians Vie for NASCAR Dads." *Washington Post*. 2 August, 2003. A1.

Coffield, Dana. "NASCAR Dads Who Voted for Bush Less Pack-Minded in '04." *Denver Post*. 20 June, 2004. L7.

Coontz, Stephanie. "Myth of the Opt-out Mom." *Christian Science Monitor*. 30 March, 2006.

Coontz, Stephanie. "Not Much Sense in Those Census Stories." *Washington Post*. 15, July 2001. B3

Dine, Philip. "Candidates Court Blue-Collar Crowd." *St. Louis Dispatch*. 28 October, 2004. A1.

Dionne, E. J. Jr., and Saundra Torry. "Quayle Recasts 'Family Values' in Terms of Domestic Policy; Vice President Says Democrats' Approach Differs." *Washington Post*. 28 August, 1992. A18.

Elder, Janet. "Soccer and Security Moms Unite." *New York Times*. 19 September, 2007.

Exum, David. "Bush Needs NASCAR Dads to Hold Fast." *Boston Herald*. 19 September, 2004. 18.

Feldman, Linda. "Why Women Are Edging Toward Bush." *Christian Science Monitor.* 23 September, 2004. 1.

Feldman, Linda. "GOP Spoke of Soccer Moms, Democrats Spoke to Them." *Christian Science Monitor.* 13 November, 1996. 3.

Gregg, Gary L. "Bubba Don't Windsurf." *National Review.* 30 September, 2004.

Hallet, Joe. "'Waitress Moms' Seen as Voters Worth Wooing." *Columbus Dispatch.* 14 October, 2000. 1A.

Harden, Blaine. "Numbers Drop for the Married with Children: Institution Becoming the Choice of the Educated, Affluent." *Washington Post.* 4 March, 2005. A3.

Harris, John F. "Clinton Pulls Punches; Ads Land Them; TV Spot Hits Dole on Family Leave as President Pitches Welfare Overhaul." *Washington Post.* 11 September, 1996. A10.

Henneberger, Melinda. "Want Votes with That? Get the 'Waitress Moms.'" *New York Times.* 25 October, 1998. Section 4, 3.

James, Susan Donaldson. "Census 2010: One-Quarter of Gay Couples Raising Children." *ABC News.* June 23, 2011. http://abcnews.go.com/Health/sex-couples-census-data-trickles-quarter-raising-children/story?id=13850332.

James, Susan Donaldson. "'Gayby Boom' Fueled by Same-Sex Parents." *ABC News.* August 3, 2009. http://abcnews.go.com/Health/ReproductiveHealth/story?id=8232392&page=1.

Jonsson, Patrik. "Dems Target 'NASCAR Dads.'" *Christian Science Monitor.* 12 September, 2003. 3.

Kahn, Joseph P. "Poll Positions 'NASCAR Dads' Are Gearing Up for the Races—Auto and Presidential." *Boston Globe.* 13 September, 2003. C1.

Klein, Joe. "How Soccer Moms Became Security Moms." *Time.* 10 February, 2003. 23.

Klinkner, Philip A. "Deflating the 'Security Moms' Angle." *Newsday.* 4 October, 2004. A45.

Kornblut, Anne E., and Michael D. Shear. "Military Moms May Be a Force at the Polls." *Washington Post.* 29 August, 2007. A6.

Kotkin, Joel, and William Frey. "Parent Trap." *The New Republic Online.* www.tnr.com/doc.mhtml?pt=3KzRTBxZkbnZ3RuM0cWdfh%3D%3D. (Accessed February 8, 2005).

Langer, Gary. "Driving the Election? Speculation That 'NASCAR Dads' Will Decide the 2004 Vote May Be Off Track." *ABC News.* http://abcnews.go.com/sections/Politics/ThisWeek/nascar_dads_040215.html. (Accessed July 14, 2004).

Lawrence, Jill. "Democrats Looking for a Ride to Office with Suburban Dads." *USA Today.* 22 May, 2002. 9A.

Leonhardt, David. "Children, the Littlest Politicians." *New York Times.* 19 February, 2006. 14.

Levin, Yuval. "Putting Parents First." *Weekly Standard.* Volume 12, Issue 12. 4 December, 2006.

Lowry, Rich. "Momma Gets Tough." *National Review.* 29 September, 2004.

Marinucci, Carla. "Candidates Courting Niche Groups for Votes." *San Francisco Chronicle.* 26 October, 2004. A4.

Marinucci, Carla. "Move Over Soccer Moms—Here Come the 'Office Park Dads." *San Francisco Chronicle.* 13 August, 2002. A1.

Mason, Julie. "National Security a Top Issue Among Women Voters for 2004." *Houston Chronicle.* 17 December, 2003. A1.

Milbank, Dana. "Deeply Divided Country Is United in Anxiety." *Washington Post.* 4 November, 2004. A28.

Morin, Richard, and Dan Balz. "'Security Mom' Bloc Proves Hard to Find." *Washington Post.* 1 October, 2004. A5.

Pear, Robert. "Married and Single Parents Spending More Time with Children, Study Finds." *New York Times.* 17 October, 2006.

Rauch, Jonathan. 2001. "The Widening Marriage Gap: America's New Class Divide." *The Atlantic Online.*

Roberts, Sam. "Most Children Still Live in Two-Parent Homes, Census Bureau Reports." *New York Times.* 21 February, 2008.

Roberts, Sam. "51% of Women Now Living without a Spouse." *New York Times.* 16 January, 2007.

Romano, Lois. "Female Support for Kerry Slips." *Washington Post.* 23 September, 2004. A7.

Rowat, Alison. "From NASCAR Dads to MTV Mob: The Ten Tribes That Will Decide the US Election." *Herald.* 25 October, 2004. 7.

Sailer, Steve. "Baby Gap: How Birthrates Color the Electoral Map." *The American Conservative.* 20 December, 2004. www.amconmag.com/2004_12_20/print/coverprint.html. (Accessed February 8, 2005).

Sandalow, Marc. "Democrats' Dilemma: How to Take Back the Nation." *San Francisco Chronicle.* 5 December, 2004. A1.

Schwartz, Maralee. "Clinton Proposes 6-Point Program to Aid Families; Candidate Faults Both GOP, Democrats on 'Family Values." *Washington Post.* 22 May, 1992. A20.

Shepard, Scott. "NASCAR Dads: GOP's Inside Track." *Atlanta Journal and Constitution.* 31 August, 2003. 1A.

Shepard, Scott. "'Waitress Moms,' Not Soccer Moms, May Decide Fall Elections." *Atlanta Constitution.* 25 October, 1998. 8A.

Shellenbarger, Sue. "When 20-Somethings Move Back Home, It Isn't All Bad." *Wall Street Journal.* 21 May, 2008. D1.

Sidoti, Liz. "GOP Losing Advantage with Married Moms." *YahooNews.*
    http://news.yahoo.com/s/ap/20061009/ap_on_el_ge/married_
    moms&printer=1;_ylt=AvF.(Accessed on October 10, 2006).
St. George, Donna. "Despite 'Mommy Guilt' Time with Kids Increasing:
    Society's Pressures, Own Expectations Alter Priorities." *Washington
    Post.* 20 March, 2007. A1.
Starr, Alexandra. "'Security Moms': An Edge for Bush?" *Business Week
    Online.* 1 December, 2003. www.businessweek.com:/print/maga-
    zine/content/03_48/b3860069.htm?mz. (Accessed on June 4, 2004).
Steinberg, Dan. "Bush Is Expected at NASCAR Race." *Washington Post.*
    14 September, 2004. D2.
Straub, Noelle. "The Presidential Debates." *Boston Herald.* 1 October,
    2004. 7.
Sweet, Lynn. "Courting the Ladies." *Chicago Sun-Times.* 13 October,
    2004a.72.
Sweet, Lynn. "Did the Women's Vote Count? How the Vote Split in Illinois,
    Nation." *Chicago Sun-Times.* 10 November, 2004b. 60.
Taber, Carol A. "How 9/11 Transformed Women Voters." *Boston Globe.* 7
    October, 2004. A23.
Tierney, John. "W. M.'s Seek S. F.'s for Fall Affair." *New York Times.* A24.
    6 June, 2004.
Todd, Chuck. "In Search of the Swing Voter." *New York Times.* 29 Decem-
    ber, 2003. A17.
Toner, Robin. "Women Feeling Freer to Suggest 'Vote for Mom.'" *New York
    Times.* 29 January, 2007.
VandeHei, Jim. "Republicans Losing the 'Security Moms.'" *Washington
    Post.* 18 August, 2006. A1.
Von Drehle, David. "For Democrats, Key Voters May Be Married to Soccer
    Moms; Pollster Says Party Should Target Office Park Dads." *Wash-
    ington Post.* 22 May, 2002. A8.
Wells, Matt. "Winning Over the NASCAR Dads." *BBC News.* www.newsv-
    ot.bbc.co.uk/mpapps/pagetools/print/news.bbc.co.uk/1/hi/world/
    americas/313. (Accessed on July 14, 2004).
Whitehead, Barbara Dafoe. "The Marriage Gap: When Will Democrats
    Wake Up?" *Commonweal.* 17 December, 2004.10.
Wisecup, Trent. "The Democrats' Marketing Mistake." *Daily Standard.* 29
    November, 2004.

Index

Abortion, 43, 59, 99; effects of parenthood on views of, 83, 84*tab*, 85*fig*, 106, 107*tab*; funding cuts and, 40; polarization of parties over, 4
African Americans: disconnect between marriage and children, 14; egalitarian orientations for non-married parents, 97; in government assistance programs, 15; higher rates of single parenthood among, 97; lower rates of marriage among, 14, 97; non-marital births, 14
Aid to Families with Dependent Children, 35
American National Election Studies, 7, 70, 98

Baby gap, 5
Bush, George H.W.: State of the Union address, 35; vetoes Family and Medical Leave Act, 42
Bush, George W., 36*tab*, 123; endorsement of ban on gay marriage, 38; inaugural address, 30; rallies support/defense for wars, 40; tax cuts by, 38; use of family-parent references by, 28, 35, 40

Carter, Jimmy: use of family-parent references by, 41
Children: as center of parents' lives, 19, 20; disadvantaged, 58; fewer married people having, 95; liberalizing political effects of raising, 6; more single people having, 95; out-of-wedlock, 14, 39, 95; parental time spent with, 2, 11, 24; protection from societal influences, 3; regulations protecting, 57, 57*fig*
Children's Health Initiative Program (CHIP), 42
Christian Coalition, 15
Clinton, Bill, 2, 23, 44; on child support, 44; convention speeches, 41, 44; inaugural address, 31; passes Family and Medical Leave Act, 42; proposals to increase parental authority on cultural influences, 44, 45; State of the Union address, 29, 30, 36*tab*, 37*tab*, 41, 45; use of family-parent references by, 29, 30, 41, 42, 45, 59; welfare reform and, 43, 44

Death penalty: comparison of parental views of, 84*tab*, 86

161